100 Favorite BIBLE PRAYERS

Stacy Edwards

THOMAS NELSON
Since 1798

CONTENTS

INTRODUCTION

Favorite Bible Prayers

Now this is the confidence that we have in Him, that
if we ask anything according to His will, He hears us.

1 JOHN 5:14

Where do we turn in times of turmoil? Whom do we praise in moments of joy? As Christians, we take both our pain and praise to God in prayer, knowing that in His presence we find the One who knows and understands us completely. We've all experienced times when someone didn't share our happiness like we had hoped. And we've certainly had plenty of miserable comforters (Job 16:2). It is never that way with God. He is our Father, comforter, provider, and creator, and His ear is always open to our cries. We can pour our hearts out to Him without pretense.

There is something so intimate about the words uttered in prayer from the lips of God's people. Whether they are moments of intense pain or extreme joy, we can be completely open and vulnerable before Him. One of the many gifts of Scripture is our ability to be a silent witness to some of the most fervent prayers of the saints. Pleas for God's protection, provision, and presence accompanied by prayers of

praise and worship echo across generations and encourage us today.

As Solomon taught us, "There is nothing new under the sun." That knowledge can bring great comfort as it reminds us that, whatever we are currently experiencing, God has walked with someone else through the same thing. Whether we are praying for physical protection like David, or for a child like Hannah, or for wisdom like Solomon, we can read the prayers of others and know that we are not alone. We are reminded time and again of God's faithfulness and steadfast love toward His people.

In *100 Favorite Bible Prayers*, we are able to step into the stories of men and women who experienced struggles and successes, battles and bewilderment, failures and fear, and who turned to God in the midst of it all. We find God faithful to answer their cries for forgiveness, restoration, comfort, and more. Their words give us hope that we can also overcome obstacles and survive trials. We are convicted by their honesty and humility as we read their pleas for forgiveness. Each prayer points us to God who hears every word.

Thank You, Father, for these prayers preserved for us within the pages of Your Word. Help us to remember that these are not simply stories. They are snapshots of real people who experienced real emotions. May the words of these men and women turn our hearts to You.

1

Psalm 19:14

Let the *words* of

my mouth and the

meditation of my

heart be acceptable

in Your sight, O Lord,

my *strength* and

my Redeemer.

GOSPEL IN, GOSPEL OUT

*E*ach of us has probably received this instruction at some point: "If you don't have something nice to say, then don't say anything at all." It's sound advice, to be sure. After all, many hearts have been hurt and relationships ruined over words that should have never been said.

While we should strive for wisdom when using our words, David's prayer reflected that he knew God desired much more from His people. It was while examining David's brothers as potential candidates for the throne, in fact, that the Lord told Samuel, "Man looks at the outward appearance, but the Lord looks at the heart" (1 Samuel 16:7). Knowing this, David desired that both his words *and* thoughts would all be pleasing to the Lord.

We have all used our words to wound, and we all undoubtedly have had thoughts that did not honor the Lord. So, what is the solution? To paraphrase another parental axiom—garbage in, garbage out—Scripture tells us, "Gospel in, gospel out." Jesus taught in Luke 6:45 that a man speaks from the overflow of his heart. In other words, what is in our hearts will come out of our mouths. Perhaps this is why we are instructed to meditate on Scripture day and night.

Like David, let us pray that our thoughts and our words, our motives and our actions, our attitudes toward Him and toward our neighbors are all acceptable in His sight.

Father, thank You for Your guidance and life-giving Scripture. May the words I speak today be like a balm to someone's aching soul.

2

Acts 4:29-30

Now, Lord, look on their threats, and grant to Your servants that with all *boldness* they may speak Your word, by stretching out Your hand to *heal*, and that signs and *wonders* may be done through the name of Your *holy* servant Jesus.

PRAYER FOR BOLDNESS

*P*eter and John found themselves being persecuted and threatened with imprisonment. Yet, there in the midst of an angry crowd, they proclaimed the name of Jesus. Because of that boldness, those in the crowd knew that these men had spent time with Jesus (Acts 4:13).

After hearing the testimony of Peter and John, their friends and fellow believers prayed for the same kind of boldness. God heard and answered that prayer, and—filled with the Holy Spirit and boldness—the disciples continued to speak the Word of God (v. 31).

Aren't you just in awe of those men? They were staring into the faces of those who desired to harm them, imprison them, and kill them. At that moment, they prayed, not for safety, but for boldness to continue doing the very thing that placed them in harm's way. They desperately desired to proclaim the name of Jesus.

When we believe in the character of God, we can be bold in the face of affliction and trials. We can trust Him to be good and to do good. That may mean His protection from persecution, or it may mean His presence in the midst of persecution. We can trust Him either way.

Father, I come to You from a place of faith and not fear. I desire Your glory over my comfort. I boldly seek Your face and proclaim Your power.

3

Exodus 33:15-16

If Your *Presence* does not go
with us, do not bring us up from
here. For how then will it be
known that Your people and I
have found *grace* in Your *sight*,
except You go with us? So we
shall be separate, Your people
and I, from all the people who
are upon the *face* of the earth.

THE PRESENCE OF GOD

*T*he children of Israel had wandered for decades through the wilderness. They had grumbled and complained. They had doubted and despaired. They had even longed for the slavery they had left behind in Egypt. And, finally, they found themselves on the edge of the promised land. God had, as He had promised, led them to a place flowing with milk and honey.

But because of the people's continual stubbornness and lack of faith over the years, God told Moses that He would not be joining the children of Israel in the promised land. God led them to the edge but then said, "I will not go up among you" (Exodus 33:3 ESV). The people were devastated at the thought of losing the presence of God.

Imagine being on the precipice of receiving something you've longed for and having God say, "You can have that, but you won't have Me with it." How many of us, when faced with the same scenario, would be equally devastated? Would we, like Moses, choose the wilderness with God over the promised land without Him? Does the presence of the Lord mean that much to us?

It's easy to get caught up in our requests, needs, and preferences. There is often an endless list of hardships and heartaches to bring before the Lord.

Father, I long for Your presence more than anything else.

4

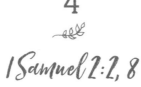

1 Samuel 2:2, 8

No one is *holy* like the LORD,
for there is none besides You,
nor is there any *rock* like our
God. . . . He *raises* the poor from
the dust and lifts the beggar
from the ash heap, to set them
among *princes* and make them
inherit the throne of glory.

NO ONE LIKE THE LORD

To be barren in Hannah's day was to live a life of disgrace. The kindest of people would have pitied her, and the cruel ones, like Peninnah, mocked and provoked her. In her prayer to the Lord, Hannah referred to her state of childlessness as an affliction from which she desperately desired relief.

Hannah's prayer highlighted God's ability to transform a person's life. She knew that He alone could take an individual from shame to celebration. From poverty to royalty. From groaning to glory. She believed in the holiness and the power of the Lord.

Every person who repents, believes the gospel, and follows Christ experiences a life-altering transformation. The change in each of us is no less miraculous than a barren woman conceiving a child. We become brand-new creations (2 Corinthians 5:17), and our hearts of stone become hearts of flesh (Ezekiel 36:26). It is a miracle and cause for celebration anytime anyone comes to know Christ.

We all go through seasons of loss, discouragement, and grief. All of us, like Hannah, have areas of pain in our lives from which we seek relief.

Lord, You are the only one able to lift us from the pit and seat us among princes. No one is holy like You, Lord.

5

2 Chronicles 20:12

For we have no *power* against
this great *multitude* that is
coming against us; nor do
we *know* what to do, but
our eyes are upon You.

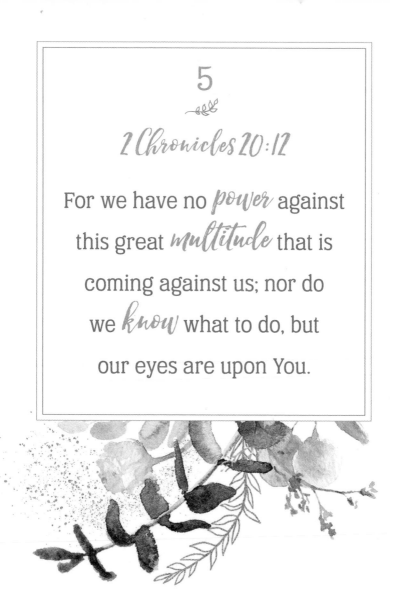

FIX OUR EYES

Jehoshaphat and his people were about to face a great enemy, and they were afraid. Armies were on their way to drive them out of the land God had given them, and Jehoshaphat did the only thing he could think to do: he prayed. In his prayer, Jehoshaphat admitted that the people were powerless to stop what was coming at them, and they simply did not know what to do.

Haven't we all, at some point in our lives, prayed a similar prayer? We've all faced a scary situation, an uncertain outcome, or a devastating diagnosis. Just like Jehoshaphat, we've experienced times when—on our own—we were powerless against what was coming at us. Hasn't each of us prayerfully uttered the words, "I don't know what to do"?

The beauty of this prayer is that, while the people didn't know what to do, they did know where to look. To focus their gaze on the enemy or themselves would have served only to heighten the people's fear and despair. They knew their only hope was to fix their eyes on God.

There will be times in our lives when we feel powerless, fearful, and uncertain as to what to do. In those moments, however, we can choose to fix our eyes on the One who can calm any storm, defeat any foe, and lead us through any valley.

Father, I fix my eyes on You as You
fill me with Your certainty.

6

Isaiah 25:1 ESV

O Lord, you are my God; I will *exalt* you; I will *praise* your name, for you have done *wonderful* things, plans formed of old, *faithful* and sure.

FAITHFUL AND SURE

God is the One who knows the end from the beginning. He is never caught off guard by our circumstances or bewildered by our behavior. He never feels pressured by the passing of time. God has always been—and will always be—in complete control of His creation.

Isaiah's acceptance of God's eternal nature, sovereignty, and faithfulness was evident in the way he prayed. He knew that God had a plan—a faithful and sure one formed long ago. Isaiah knew what Jeremiah knew: God's plans for us have been prepared in advance (Jeremiah 1:5), and they are plans to prosper us (29:11).

When we understand that God has a plan and that nothing about our existence is haphazard or out of control, it changes the way we pray. And when we understand that we were made *on purpose* and with a purpose, it changes the way we live. Each of us is intentionally and uniquely handmade by a holy God who has a plan for us.

God has proven time and again that He is able "to rescue the godly from trials" (2 Peter 2:9 ESV). He led His followers out of lions' dens, fiery furnaces, and prisons because He still had plans for those individuals. If there's still breath in your body, He isn't finished with you. Trust Him to be as He has always been: faithful and sure.

Only You, God, are worthy of my trust. You
know the plans You have made for me, and
I can rest assured in Your promise.

7

Jeremiah 15:16 ESV

Your *words* were found,
and I ate them, and
your words became
to me a *joy* and the
delight of my heart, for
I am called by your name,
O LORD, *God* of hosts.

DELIGHT OF MY HEART

A new car, a snazzier job title, that "must-have" you saw in the store the other day. These are all things that are not bad in and of themselves, but when we place too much importance on them, they can easily become more important than they should. That's when they can be considered idols. There is a lot of talk about idols in the Old Testament. It's tempting to skim over it, thinking it has little to do with us.

The prophet Isaiah described the people's worship of idols when he said that the people delighted in things that did not profit them (Isaiah 44:9). They were seeking joy in things that did not benefit them or anyone around them. They longed for things that were useless to them. Suddenly, these idols don't seem so far-fetched, do they?

Jeremiah came along and, through his prayer, reminded us where true joy and delight are found. He said that he *ate* the words of God. Imagine being so hungry for God's Word that you just want to devour it! As Jeremiah filled himself with Scripture, the words became a joy to him. What begins as a discipline can become a delight.

What are we delighting in today? What do we treasure? What do we long for? Is it, as Isaiah described, something that can't hear us when we call? Doesn't see us in our distress? Or is it, as Jeremiah described, the very Words of God that bring us joy and delight?

Lord, may we delight always and
only in You and Your Word.

8

Psalm 119:31

I *cling* to Your
testimonies;
O *Lord*, do not
put me to
shame!

CLING

*I*f you've ever watched an infant with a pacifier or a child with a favorite toy, then you know how tightly someone can cling to something. And lest we think we don't carry that habit into adulthood, imagine someone attempting to take the item you hold most dear. The fact is that we all cling to something.

The psalmist prayed to the Lord and declared that he was clinging to the words of the Lord. Could we say the same thing? In Joshua 23, there's a stern warning from Joshua to the children of Israel regarding the things they were choosing to cling to. Specifically, he warned them not to cling to the things the Lord had already delivered them from (v. 12).

What are some ways we may do that today? Maybe we look back with longing like Lot's wife (Genesis 19:24–26). Or like the children of Israel who romanticized bondage the moment freedom felt uncomfortable. We hold on to anger, bitterness, and unforgiveness, even though God has delivered us from the power of darkness (Colossians 1:13–14). The Lord is working to restore relationships, but we don't want to let go of our hurt feelings. We continue to sit in shame and refuse to embrace the grace offered to us in Christ (Zephaniah 3:19).

Father, help us to let go of the things that are harmful to our spirits and our relationship with You. We choose to cling to You and Your testimonies.

9

Job 42:5

I have *heard* of
You by the *hearing*
of the ear, but now
my eye *sees* You.

BUT NOW

*W*hen have you felt the closest to God? For many of us, it is during seasons of sorrow and suffering that we sense the nearness of Him the most. God has promised us that He will never leave us. We can always be assured of His presence, but it is often in those moments of agony that He chooses to reveal Himself in a whole new way.

Job was a man of great faith. He was described as a man who was "blameless and upright, one who feared God and turned away from evil" (Job 1:1 ESV). He made it his practice to rise early and offer prayers and sacrifices for his entire family. By all accounts, Job was a good and godly man. Yet, in his prayer, Job acknowledged that his suffering allowed him to see with his own eyes what he had always heard to be true of God.

We can all think of times when we've seen God at work with our own eyes. Maybe it was in the form of physical protection from an accident or illness that should have had a worse outcome. Or perhaps it looked like provision from an unexpected source in a time of great need. Or it may have been a person who came along at just the right moment to comfort, guide, or assist us.

We have heard of You, Lord, but now our eyes see You.

10

Psalm 5:3

My *Voice* You shall
hear in the *morning*,
O LORD; in the morning
I will direct it to *You*,
and I will look up.

PRAYING WITH EXPECTATION

Many of David's prayers are preserved for us in Scripture, and there is much that we can learn from them. In just this one sentence, for instance, David gave us three important elements of prayer.

First, David said that the Lord would hear his voice. In other words, David was going to pray. He was intentional about taking time to speak with the Lord. From this, we can learn that the first step to a healthy prayer life is simply to set aside time to pray.

Second, David directed his prayers in the right direction. He prayed to God—the One who could meet any need, heal any wound, forgive any sin, and redeem any pain. How many of us are often tempted to fix our own problems only to discover that we can't? David went to the One who had the power to help.

Finally, David said that he would look up. Why? Because he was anticipating a response from the Lord. David prayed with the expectation that his prayer was heard and that an answer was on its way. We too can pray with expectation knowing that God hears the prayers of the righteous (1 Peter 3:12).

Let's be people of prayer. May we be intentional about setting aside time specifically to speak with the Father. Let's direct our prayers to the One who cares for us. And may we pray with an expectation that God hears and will respond.

Father, only You are worthy of praise and worship. It is only Your face that I seek.

11

Psalm 51:12

Restore to me
the joy of Your
salvation, and
uphold me by Your
generous Spirit.

JOY

*H*ave you ever done something that you feared was unforgivable? Have you ever experienced intense grief over your own sin? We all have, and so did David.

Psalm 51 is so moving, especially if you understand where David had been prior to praying it. How deep the pit. How grievous the sin. How public and painful the fall from grace.

David sinned with Bathsheba. He then had her husband killed. Lie upon lie upon lie. Adultery and murder. Shame and selfishness. Pride. But then . . . prayer.

"Have mercy . . ." (v. 1).

"Wash me . . ." (v. 2).

"I know my transgressions . . ." (v. 3 ESV).

"Restore to me the joy of Your salvation."

David was still a man after God's heart. He was a sinful, fallen, prone-to-wander man, but he still belonged to the Lord. I'm moved by the realization that David believed mercy, cleansing, renewal, and joy were still available to him. There is no pit so deep that God can't lift us out. There is no sin so grievous that His grace can't cover it.

David didn't ask for his salvation to be restored because that was never taken away. He asked for his *joy* to be restored. Mercy, grace, and joy are still available for those who repent and believe. We can still come to God in prayer and ask for these things, and we can trust Him to offer them.

Thank You, Lord, that Your grace is big enough to cover over the world's sin. I rejoice in Your love and mercy!

12

Psalm 56:3-4

Whenever I am afraid, I will *trust* in You. In God (I will praise His word), in *God* I have put my trust; I will not fear. What can *flesh* do to me?

FAITH OVER FEAR

*W*e all have situations that cause us fear or anxiety. Does anyone else have the recurring dream where you're wandering around a school campus frantically trying to locate the class that you've forgotten to attend all semester? The one where you walk from building to building and hallway to hallway, but nothing and no one looks familiar?

Or is your source of fear completely different? Perhaps you worry about losing someone you love, not having enough money, or missing out on something in life. Whatever it is that causes us to fear, David's prayer gives us a way to deal with it. David declared that when fear came his way, he would choose to trust God. He would choose faith over fear.

God knows how to handle all of our feelings. Psalm 56 is a balm to the soul of anyone who has ever felt anxious, lost, afraid, sad, discouraged, rejected, overlooked, forgotten, misunderstood, or overwhelmed. If you feel that someone is oppressing you, attacking you, twisting your words, or stirring up strife, this prayer is for you.

Toward the end of this prayer, after listing all the things that caused him fear, David reminded himself that God was for him (v. 9). Whatever this day holds for us, we can know the same. Let's take a deep breath, pour a little cup of something hot, and put our trust in God.

Every breath I take, Lord, I take because of You. With each breath, I am reminded that nothing slips by You— Almighty God, Everlasting Father, Prince of Peace.

13

Isaiah 26:3

You will *keep* him in *perfect* peace, whose mind is stayed on You, because he *trusts* in You.

PRAYER OF PEACE

*W*hat does peace look like to you? A cabin in the woods? A candlelit bubble bath? Ocean waves crashing against a sandy shore? Five minutes of silence in the midst of a chaotic life? Whatever peace we think we are achieving is, at best, temporary. It only lasts until the bathwater turns cold, the storm clouds roll in, or the next drama of life occurs.

This is not the peace that Isaiah described in his prayer. There were three elements to the peace he spoke of that set it apart from what you or I might describe as "peace" today.

First, the peace of Isaiah's prayer was perfect. The Hebrew word translated as "peace" in this verse is *shalom*. The peace that Isaiah referred to was more than a momentary rest. *Shalom* means a peace that includes completeness, wellness in body and spirit, and overall harmony. It's a perfect peace.

Second, the peace Isaiah referenced was perpetual. Isaiah had the assurance that God would *keep* in perfect peace the one who would fix his or her mind on Him. He believed the peace to be ongoing and consistent regardless of circumstances.

Finally, Isaiah knew that God was the provider of this perfect and perpetual peace. When fear or anxiety attempt to take control, Isaiah's prayer reminds us that this perpetual and perfect peace is available to all who fix their minds on God.

> Father, You are the God who Sees, and you know my deepest fears and worries. I give them over to You and dwell in Your peace.

14

1 Kings 3:9

Therefore *give* to
Your servant an
understanding *heart*
to judge Your people,
that I may discern
between *good* and evil.

GOOD AND EVIL

*H*ave you ever struggled with knowing the right thing to do? Have you ever lost sleep over a decision you had to make? Or perhaps you have struggled with knowing whether someone was being genuine or trustworthy in a given situation. The reality is that the "right" choice or answer isn't always obvious.

The world is desperately trying to blur the lines between good and evil. Even those desiring to live godly lives can find themselves struggling to discern between the two. This must have also been the case in Solomon's day. When faced with an opportunity to request anything of the Lord, Solomon desired the ability to discern between good and evil.

The good versus evil dilemma continued on into Isaiah's day, and he gave a stern warning to those who would call good what God had called evil (Isaiah 5:20). Fortunately, there is a solution for those of us desiring discernment. We can, just like Solomon, ask the Lord for the wisdom needed to make godly choices in our lives. Scripture promises that those who desire wisdom need only pray for it (James 1:5).

Solomon's prayer reminds us that we are not left alone to figure out what is good and what is evil. Our hearts are deceptive and, left to our own devices, we could easily make the wrong choices. But we, like Solomon, can pray to the One who gives wisdom generously to all who seek it.

Lord of Righteousness, please give me the
guidance to walk the path of wisdom.

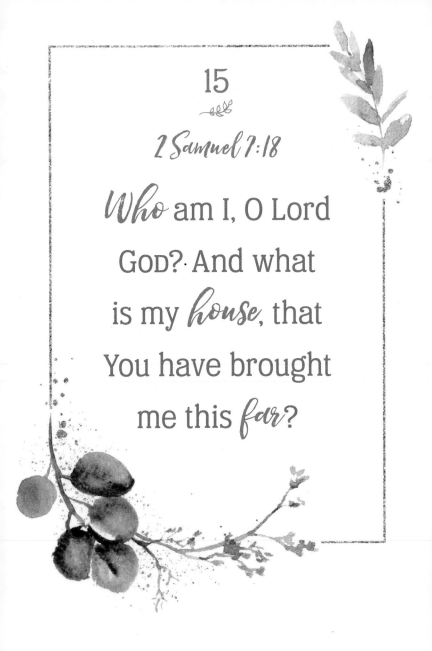

15

2 Samuel 7:18

Who am I, O Lord God? And what is my *house*, that You have brought me this *far*?

COUNT YOUR BLESSINGS

*I*t's often easier to see the negatives than the positives in our day-to-day lives. We are all too aware of the things that we wish were different. Hardships seem to loom large and demand our attention. We are all, at times, prone to complain.

What if we chose, instead, to do as the old hymn advises and count our many blessings? If we paused to list all the gifts God has given us and all the ways He has provided, it would truly surprise us what the Lord has done. We would, like David, cry out in amazement and humility at how far God has brought us.

David's prayer was one of humility because he was all too aware of his human failings. We can all certainly relate. What if we received exactly what we deserved from God? Scary thought, isn't it?

His prayer was also one of gratitude because he knew exactly who had brought him "this far." In a world where we often live with an "if it's to be, it's up to me" mentality, the reality is that all we have, all we are, and all we accomplish is because of the grace and mercy of God.

Lord, help us to be mindful of all that You've given
to us. May our prayers be marked by humility
(1 Peter 5:6) and gratitude (Philippians 4:6).

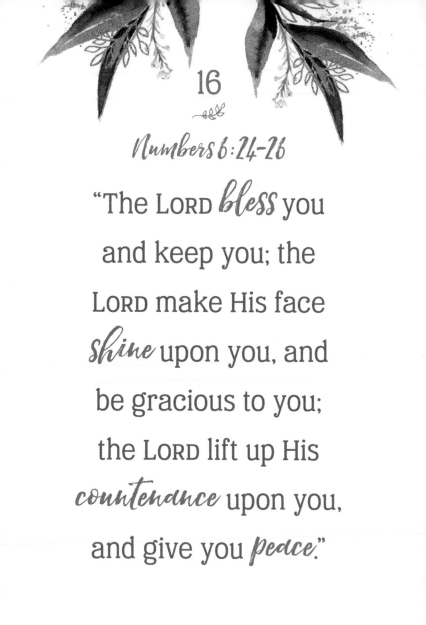

16

Numbers 6:24–26

"The LORD *bless* you and keep you; the LORD make His face *shine* upon you, and be gracious to you; the LORD lift up His *countenance* upon you, and give you *peace*."

PRAY FOR ONE ANOTHER

*H*ave you ever found yourself at a loss as to how to help someone in pain? Have you, upon hearing of someone's loss or struggle, said, "All we can do is pray"? It's probably true of all of us that we often treat prayer as a last resort. But what if that wasn't the case? What if prayer wasn't a *last* resort but, instead, was our *first* response?

Charles Spurgeon, known to many as the "Prince of Preachers," was quoted as saying that he considered someone praying for him as the greatest act of kindness. This prayer from Numbers is one of the kindest and gentlest of prayers, and it is a great prayer to pray over anyone, anytime.

This prayer was given to Moses by God, to be spoken by Aaron over the children of Israel. It included a request for the Lord's blessing, protection, presence, grace, and peace for the people. There really isn't anything else that a person could need. When we don't know what to say, this prayer really says it all.

What would happen if we sincerely spoke these words over our families, friends, neighbors, and coworkers? Just imagine how hearts would be healed and relationships restored if we prayed this prayer (and meant it) over people we have disagreed with or still harbor grudges against? We can't genuinely pray for these blessings on their behalf without a softening of our hearts taking place.

Lord, open our eyes to those around us in need of
Your presence, protection, or provision. Make us
people who pray for one another each day.

17

Psalm 9:10

And those who *know* Your name will put their *trust* in You; for You, LORD, have not forsaken those who *seek* You.

NOT FORSAKEN

*H*ave you ever placed your trust in something or someone that let you down? It can be discouraging to discover that you've misjudged a person or situation. It can also make you a little reluctant to trust again.

This prayer of David's is a beautiful reminder of the trustworthiness of our God. The first part of his prayer reminds us that while we can't know everything about God, there are things that He allows us to know about Him. David used the Hebrew word *shem*, which is translated in this prayer as *name*. According to BlueLetterBible.org, it also includes the concepts of reputation, fame, and glory. "Those who know You, Lord," David was saying, "trust You."

The second part of David's prayer tells us why that knowledge leads us to trust God. By getting to know God, His people witness the trustworthiness of His character. They see that He never forsakes, forgets, or abandons those seek Him.

We too can know God when we spend time in prayer and in the study of His Word. Then, as we get to know Him more, we will also see evidence that He does not forsake those who seek Him. We will discover that those who seek Him will find Him, and to those who knock the door will be opened (Matthew 7:7–8). Our God is trustworthy.

Thank You, Father, for being the
unshakable Rock of my Salvation.

18

Matthew 26:39

He went a little farther and fell on His face, and *prayed*, saying, "O My Father, if it is *possible*, let this cup pass from Me; nevertheless, not as I will, but as *You* will."

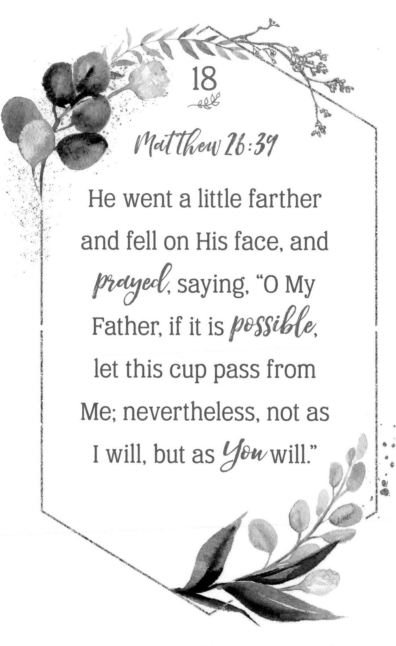

THE WILL OF THE FATHER

*I*n our flesh, we all want our own ways. I think I know best, you think you know best, and the truth is that neither of us do. But it's so difficult to let go of what little control we think we have over our lives. We try to take the reins and—let's be honest—we don't even know what's going on half the time.

Jesus, on the other hand, knew exactly what was about to happen. He was acutely aware of the betrayal, mockery, and pain He was about to endure. If there were any other way to accomplish the work He had come to do, He was willing to let the cup of God's wrath pass Him by. But there wasn't any other way, so Jesus submitted His will to the will of the Father.

Jesus was obedient to the point of death on a cross (Philippians 2:8). His desire was to do the work God had sent Him to do, which was to make a way for sinful man to have access to the Almighty. His prayer of anguish and humility makes clear His devotion to the Father and His love for us.

Most of us, Lord, will never be asked to sacrifice to such an extent. At most, we endure mild discomfort and momentary trials for the sake of Your name. Give us the humility and courage, however, to pray, "Not as I will, but as You will."

19

Psalm 143:12

In Your *mercy* cut
off my enemies, and
destroy all those who
afflict my soul; for I
am Your *servant*.

I AM YOUR SERVANT

Do you ever wake up in the middle of the night feeling anxious and overwhelmed? Does the weight of the world seem to rest, at times, squarely on your shoulders? We can take comfort in knowing that the men and women in Scripture also felt the same way. David prayed Psalm 143 during a particularly difficult season in his life.

David described his spirit as overwhelmed and his heart as distressed. He felt persecuted and crushed (vv. 3–4). We've all known discouragement, disappointment, and distress. How can we respond when we feel this way? As we see in Psalm 143, David chose to pray.

His prayer laid his requests before the Lord. "Answer me," he cried. "Do not hide Your face from me. . . . Deliver me. . . . Teach me. . . . Lead me" (vv. 7–10). We can sense the desperation rising as he poured out his heart to God. Then, suddenly, David's prayer came to a screeching halt with the reminder that God is merciful and that David belonged to Him.

When life seems too much to handle, prayer has a way of reminding us of who God is and where we stand in relation to Him. He is merciful and able to destroy any who come against His servants. In the New Testament, Peter reaffirms this when he says, "The Lord knows how to rescue the godly from trials" (2 Peter 2:9 ESV). Whatever we are dealing with, we belong to God and He knows how to take care of us.

Here I am, Lord. Send me out into my day with the kind of confidence and courage that can only come from You.

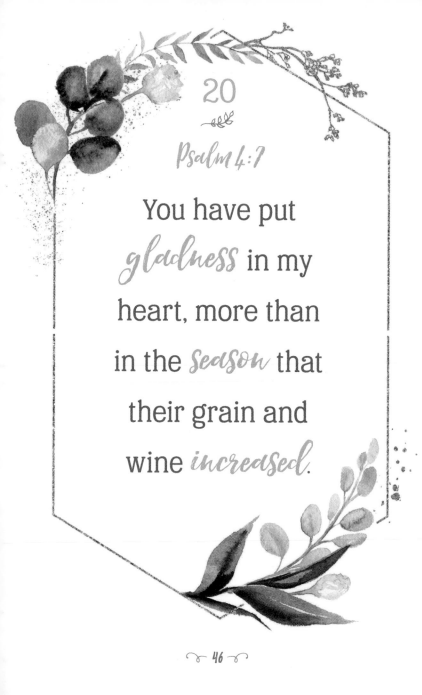

20

Psalm 4:7

You have put *gladness* in my heart, more than in the *season* that their grain and wine *increased*.

GLADNESS FROM GOD

*W*orldly happiness is this elusive thing that many of us spend our days chasing after. We seek it through possessions, relationships, and achievements. There are moments when we think we have captured it, but as soon as our circumstances change, it slips away again.

The gladness that David spoke of in this prayer is something very different. First and foremost, it has a different source. David knew that it came from the Lord. "*You* have put gladness in my heart," he prayed to God. When the *source* of our joy is constant, then our joy is also constant. God said of Himself, "I do not change" (Malachi 3:6).

David compared the gladness he received from the Lord to the two things that the people of his time would have equated with worldly happiness. He mentioned grain, which would have meant provision for the people. And he also mentioned wine, which indicated prosperity. Aren't we the same today? We call ourselves "happy" if our physical needs are met and, if a little extra is thrown in, all the better.

But David said that the gladness the Lord gave him was more than provision and prosperity. His gladness didn't depend on how well the crops did that year. It wasn't dependent on the weather, the whim of another person, or anything he himself achieved. His gladness came from God. And that alone made it *more*.

Father, may my smile beam Your love,
blessing all those around me today.

21

2 Kings 6:17

And Elisha prayed, and said, "Lord, I *pray*, open his eyes that he may see." Then the Lord *opened* the eyes of the young man, and he saw. And behold, the *mountain* was full of horses and *chariots* of fire all around Elisha.

OPEN OUR EYES

*W*e have all had seasons of struggling when we felt like no one noticed. Or we have realized, after the fact, that someone close to us was hurting and we never even knew. Perhaps we have become focused on all that we wish we had and have become blinded to our blessings. Whatever the scenario, we have all, at some point, been blinded to the reality of a situation.

In 2 Kings 6:16–20, there is a battle taking place. On two separate occasions, Elisha prayed that the Lord would open the eyes of the people. They were afraid because they didn't see the presence and protection of the Lord. But when God opened their eyes, they saw it clearly.

What if we prayed for God to open our eyes? Maybe we would begin truly seeing the people around us. That person who stops to speak to us when we're already running late? The lady sitting alone at a social event? The guy we avoid because he looks, acts, or thinks differently than us?

> Open our eyes, Lord, that we may see. Help
> us to see individuals and not inconveniences.
> May we see opportunities and not obstacles.
> Open our eyes, Lord, that we may see You.

22

Psalm 139:23 24

Search me, O God, and
know my *heart*; try me, and
know my anxieties; and
See if there is any wicked
way in me, and lead me
in the way *everlasting*.

FULLY KNOWN

*I*t's often difficult to be our true selves in this social media world with its filtered photographs and cropped images. We may fear being rejected by others if they knew all of our behind-the-scenes realities. We gladly share pictures of our toes in the sand, but are hesitant to admit there are often tears in the shower. However, these superficial relationships are never satisfying or sanctifying.

In Psalm 139, David prayed that God would thoroughly search him, truly know his heart, and reveal to him any areas of disobedience. He could have this intimate, soul-baring experience with God because he was confident of God's love for him. David found comfort in the knowledge that nothing about him was hidden from the One who created him.

Scripture tells us that God demonstrated His love by sending His Son to die for us while we were still sinners (Romans 5:8). God sees us at our worst. He knows all that we have done, are doing, and will do in the future. His love is not dependent on us cleaning up our act, ridding our lives of the drama, or digging ourselves out of the pit. He knows us and He loves us.

We don't have to fear being fully known by God because we are also fully loved. Let's desire to go deeper with the Lord.

Search us, Father. Know our hearts.

23

1 Samuel 1:11

Then she made a *vow* and
said, "O LORD of hosts, if
You will *indeed* look on the
affliction of Your maidservant
and *remember* me, and not
forget Your maidservant, but
will give Your maidservant
a male child, then I will *give*
him to the LORD all the days
of his *life*, and no razor
shall come upon his head."

PRAYER OF FAITH

*I*t's easy to read about the men and women in Scripture and minimize their struggles and suffering. We often know how their stories end, yet we forget that they did not know. Their concerns, fears, and faith were genuine. Hannah's prayer for a child is an example of a faith that persevered.

We see in 1 Samuel 1:2 that she was childless, and by verse 20 of that same chapter, she had a son. While we may read her story in one sitting, we must remember that this was a long journey of faith for her. She was barren in a culture that considered childlessness a thing of shame. She was mocked and harassed for years (v. 7). Yet she still prayed to the Lord for the desire of her heart, believing that He was able to fulfill it.

We all know what it's like to wait on the Lord. We live in a world governed by time, and we often feel panic when we think too much time has passed without our prayers being addressed the way we would prefer. But God is not bound by time. It is never too late for Him to act on our behalf.

What is the prayer in your life that the Enemy would have you give up on? Maybe you're in need of physical healing, financial provision, or the restoration of a relationship. Whatever the need, we can learn from Hannah's prayer that it's never too late for God to intervene.

Father, You know the deepest desires of my heart.
May I have the courage to keep this dream alive
and the patience to wait for Your perfect timing.

24

Psalm 145:5

I will meditate
on the *glorious*
splendor of
Your majesty,
and on Your
wondrous works.

PRAYER OF PRAISE

*H*ave you ever found yourself at a loss for words when you sit down to pray? It could be that you are so heartbroken over a situation that you don't know what to say. Too often, our prayer lives become repetitive and we simply don't have any fresh words to use. We desire the presence, provision, and protection of the Lord, but we feel like it has all been said a thousand times before.

This prayer of David's can help breathe new life into our time with the Lord. It reminds us of an element that we often leave out. Praise. How many of us are guilty of rushing into our prayer time with our laundry list of needs? Or how often do we hurry through our prayers without *meditating* as David mentioned?

David said that, in his prayer, he would meditate on two specific things: God's character and His works. In other words, David was reminding himself of what he knew to be true of God and of all the things God had done. Consider how much more elaborate our prayers would be if we spent time on just those two things! We will never be at a loss for words if we take our cues from David's prayer and focus on the character and goodness of our God.

Thank You. Thank You. Thank You. Father,
You alone are worthy of our praise.

25

Jeremiah 32:17

Ah, Lord GOD! *Behold,*
You have made the
heavens and the earth
by Your great *power*
and outstretched arm.
There is *nothing*
too hard for You.

NOTHING TOO HARD

Sometimes we just need a reminder. We need to take a step back from the situation, be still, and know (Psalm 46:10) that God is still in complete control of His creation. He is the Lord. Is anything too hard for Him? (Spoiler alert: the answer is no.)

The Enemy is always on the prowl looking for someone to devour, and he often uses despair to do it. He wants people to feel hopeless, but Paul described God as the "God of hope" (Romans 15:13). Just look at all God promised to the people in Jeremiah 33:6–14.

Healing. Restoration. Cleansing. Forgiveness. And—wait for it—joy where there had been only desolation. Peace and prosperity where there had only been "waste" (vv. 6–10 ESV).

Whatever your need is today, God can meet it. He is still in the healing, restoring, cleansing, and forgiving business. And if you find yourself today in a desolate place and you wonder if it will ever change, listen to the words of the Lord:

"Behold, I am the LORD, the God of all flesh. Is there anything too hard for Me?" (32:27).

Lord, only You know what I truly need today.
Only You know what I can handle today. Only
You have laid out Your perfect plans for my day.
May I meet today with wonder and praise.

26

Psalm 131:1

LORD, my *heart* is not haughty, nor my *eyes* lofty. Neither do I concern myself with *great* matters, nor with things too *profound* for me.

PRAYER OF TRUST

*H*ave you ever asked God, "Why?" Maybe when a tragedy occurred or a prayer wasn't answered the way you had hoped. Or have you wondered, "How?" How is God going to bring any good from your particular circumstance? There are things about God we will never understand. God told us that His ways and thoughts are higher than ours just as the heavens are higher than the earth (Isaiah 55:9).

That brings us to this short and simple prayer of David. David accepted his position before the Lord and trusted the Lord to take care of him. He would not demand an explanation from God nor would he attempt to understand all the ways of God. David was comfortable with the realization that there were things "too profound" for him.

Don't we often fall into the trap of frustration when we can't figure God out? We desperately desire to know all the ins and outs of His plans, how everything will all come together, and what it means for us. But when we think like this, we greatly underestimate the greatness of our God.

We should certainly strive to know all we can know about God. And there are aspects of His divine character and will that He graciously reveals to us. Like David, though, let's also learn to be comfortable not knowing what we can't know and trust that the Lord is in complete control.

> Father, I don't always know why or how or
> where or when. I can rest assured that You
> have all the answers and are in control.

27

Acts 1:24-25

And they prayed and said, "You, O Lord, who know the *hearts* of all, show which of these two You have *chosen* to take part in this *ministry* and *apostleship* from which Judas by transgression fell, that he might go to his own *place.*"

BIG DECISIONS

What is our initial reaction when an important decision must be made? Maybe we weigh the pros and cons of the various options. Perhaps we speculate on the response we might receive from other people. We may even spend some sleepless nights worrying about making the right choice.

When it came time to choose a man to serve among them, the apostles spent time in prayer. They didn't take a poll among themselves or choose the guy with the most connections in the community. They sought counsel from the only One who knew the heart of every man. They desired the one God had chosen.

There are several possible responses when we are faced with the responsibility of making an important choice of some kind. We could panic as we analyze the possible repercussions of our decision. We could procrastinate, which always adds a little more stress to an already stressful situation.

Or we can choose to do what the eleven apostles did. We can pray. We can seek to be responsible in the decisions we make. After all, they had narrowed the decision down to two men who met all their requirements (vv. 21–23). In the end, what mattered most was who God had chosen. What big decisions do you need to bring before the Lord today?

Lord, You know all of my decisions, big and small.
Today I ask for wisdom to know when to be still
and when to act on each decision, and may all of
my decisions be for Your glory and honor.

28

Psalm 22:3-4

But You are *holy*, enthroned in the *praises* of Israel. Our fathers *trusted* in You; they trusted, and You *delivered* them.

YOU ARE HOLY

*P*salm 22 shows us the beautiful progression of prayer. David began in pain and ended with praise. And all throughout the prayer, he continually reminded himself of what he knew to be true of God. This prayer is a perfect example of how spending time speaking with the Lord calms our spirits in times of trouble.

David opened his prayer by pouring out his feelings to God (vv. 1–2) and telling Him about his struggles (vv. 6–8). In the midst of it all, David recalled the past faithfulness of God to His people (vv. 4–5) and God's faithfulness to David personally (vv. 9–10). It's as if, in response to his concerns, the Lord reminded David of who was in control.

Perhaps the most beautiful part of the prayer is that it ended with David's certainty regarding God's intervention. As he was reminded of God's character and faithfulness, David's prayer became filled with the expectation that God would answer.

We can learn a great deal about prayer and suffering by reading David's words. We know that God cares about our feelings and that we can come to Him with them. Yet we should always view our circumstances (and our feelings about them) in light of what we know to be true about God—He is holy, and He will deliver those who love Him.

> Holy, holy, holy, You are Lord God Almighty.
> Purifiy my heart, Lord, may it be like Yours.

29

Psalm 86:11 (NKJV)

Teach me Your
way, O Lord;
I will walk in
Your truth.

ONE STEP AT A TIME

*W*hy did David pray to be taught the ways and the paths of the Lord? And why did Solomon, David's son, also desire to follow those same paths? Solomon advised his own son to "acknowledge" God in all his ways so that the Lord would "direct" his "paths," (Proverbs 3:6). When we follow the ways of the Lord, we can know that we are walking toward our desired destination.

Every act of obedience, every step of faith, every denial of self, every act of love, every time we have trusted in the midst of turmoil, every time we have chosen faith over fear—they've all been steps on this straight path. Every one of those choices has led us one step closer to glory.

We don't need to look back at what was or what might have been. It's a waste of our time to look side to side to see what others are doing better or differently than us, who seems to be having an easier time, or who is mocking the path that we've chosen.

Proverbs 4:25 instructs us to keep our eyes straight ahead. We need to simply stay in our own lanes and remain focused on what God has called us to do. Scripture encourages us to run the race set before us. Whatever we're going through today, let's choose to stay on the Lord's path. Let's keep moving forward. God is leading us home one step at a time, and He will make every step count.

Father, guide my steps as I walk the path
that brings me closer to You.

30

Psalm 18:1-2

I will *love* You, O LORD, my strength. The LORD is my rock and my *fortress* and my deliverer; my God, my *strength*, in whom I will trust; my shield and the horn of my salvation, my *stronghold*.

RELIABLE DEFENDER

*O*ne great way to begin a prayer is to declare our love for the Lord and then describe all that He has done in an area of our lives. We see this pattern in many of David's prayers. In this particular prayer, David focused on the ways God had physically protected him from his enemies.

Over the course of his life, David had seen the Lord's mighty hand at work many times. In the prayer found in Psalm 18, he recounted the ways God had intervened in times of danger and had rescued him from the hands of his enemies. David declared that, at one point, he cried out to the Lord because he knew that death was imminent (18:4) and the Lord delivered him (v. 17).

What David knew about the Lord is that He was a reliable defender. Time and again, David called and the Lord answered. God was his rock; He was steady. He was David's fortress; He was strong. God was his deliverer; He was able to save. David had experienced it in his own life and could, with confidence, pray, "My God, in whom I trust."

Certainly we could all think of times when we have experienced the steadfastness, strength, and salvation of the Lord. If we looked back over our lives, we would all, like David, be able to recall times when God graciously intervened. Once our eyes are opened to all that He has done, our prayers will be full of praise for our reliable defender.

Thank You, Father, for intervening in my life. You are my reliable defender, my mighty fortress.

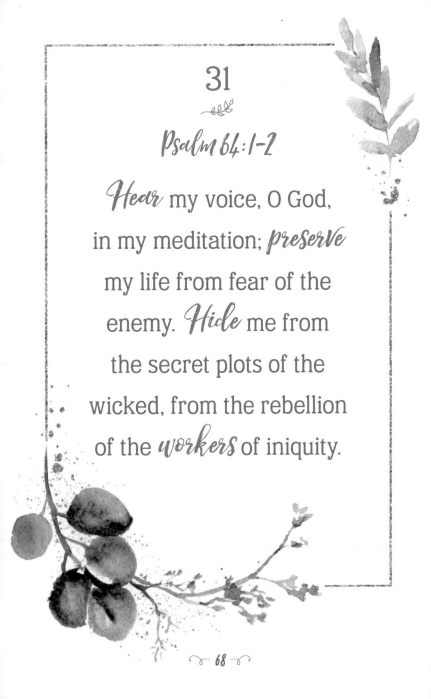

31

Psalm 64:1-2

Hear my voice, O God,
in my meditation; *preserve*
my life from fear of the
enemy. *Hide* me from
the secret plots of the
wicked, from the rebellion
of the *workers* of iniquity.

HEAR, HELP, HIDE

*W*e don't all experience the same needs at the same time. There are, as Peter described, "various trials," (1 Peter 1:6). One person may be experiencing financial struggles while another is dealing with relational difficulties. Someone may be praying for physical healing while someone else is asking for peace of mind.

This prayer highlights three specific needs that we all, at some point, have experienced and will likely experience again. First, David prayed, "Hear my voice, O God." Have you ever just needed to know that you were being heard?

Second, David asked the Lord to help him. We have all been in situations where we desperately desired God to move. There are times when the circumstances demand far more than our human efforts can accomplish.

Third, David prayed, "Hide me." The same God who blinded the eyes of Saul could blind the eyes of those who sought to harm David. How often do we try to limit the power of our God? The man after God's own heart believed that He was able to hide him, and David was bold enough to ask for it.

Our prayers will become bolder as our view of God becomes bigger. When we get a glimpse of His power in our lives, we will find ourselves praying, "Hear me, help me, hide me," types of prayers.

> Father, You are the Master Over All, including my own various trials. Help me to hear Your voice.

32

Psalm 72:16 ESV

May there be *abundance* of grain in the land; on the tops of the mountains may it wave; may its *fruit* be like Lebanon; and may people *blossom* in the cities like the grass of the field!

PRAYER FOR OUR COMMUNITIES

*H*ow many of our prayers are focused on—or are on behalf of—people outside of our immediate circles? Let's think about it for a moment. Are we, on a regular basis, pleading for the salvation, protection, and blessing of folks that we may not even know by name? The cashier at the market, the guy at the hardware store, or the neighbor who plays his music a little too loudly? If we are loving our neighbor as commanded, wouldn't that include praying for them?

In Psalm 72, Solomon is praying for the future heir of David's line. He prayed that the king would be honored by the people and that he would be a kind and compassionate leader. Solomon prays for the future king, but he also prays for the people in the cities to blossom.

The Lord speaks this same concept through the prophet Jeremiah when He says, "Seek the welfare of the city . . . for in its welfare you will find your welfare" (Jeremiah 29:7 ESV). We, as individuals, will blossom when our communities, as a whole, blossom. And this will occur only when we begin actively seeking the welfare of those who live among us.

Let's look around our communities. What can we do to help those who are barely surviving begin to thrive? Wouldn't it be wonderful to look around and see our cities prospering and our fellow citizens blossoming?

Thank You, Lord, for my family, friends, and neighbors.
Help me to blossom in my community, showing
kindness and compassion to everyone I meet.

33

Exodus 15:6

Your right hand, O Lord,
has become *glorious* in
power; Your right hand,
O Lord, has *dashed*
the enemy in pieces.

GLORIOUS IN POWER

The children of Israel found themselves between the proverbial rock and a hard place. Specifically, they were caught with the Red Sea before them and the Egyptian army approaching from the rear. Just when they thought all hope was lost, the Lord breathed on the waters. God parted the Red Sea, and they walked across on dry ground.

Following this display of His power, Moses prayed a prayer of praise to God emphasizing His might and majesty. All it took was a single blast from His nostrils and the water piled up on the sides, making way for God's people (Exodus 15:8). What an unforgettable sight that would have been!

Yet we have seen God do equally amazing things and are often prone to forget. Haven't we all faced scenarios where we doubted that anything could be done to help? Don't we sometimes label a situation as hopeless, as if we don't serve a God who saved an entire people by simply breathing?

The God who hears our prayers is glorious in power. He is known for parting waters and dashing enemies to pieces. As we pray, let's remember all the ways God has made His power known in our circumstances. No matter how hopeless a situation may seem, all we need is for God to breathe out His glorious power.

Creator of all, Father, how magnificent is Your power!

34

1 Kings 19:4

But he himself went a day's *journey* into the wilderness, and came and sat down under a broom tree. And he *prayed* that he might die, and said, "It is enough! Now, LORD, take my *life*, for I am no better than my fathers!"

AN HONEST PRAYER

How often are we completely honest with the people in our lives? Do we tell them every time we wake up feeling blue for no reason? Do we confess that things just aren't going our way? Are we comfortable confessing our sins or admitting the ways our lives just haven't turned out like we hoped?

The greater likelihood is that we tell people what we think they want to hear and what we believe they can handle. After all, we don't want to be that person. The one that always has the drama and is avoided by others.

The beautiful thing about prayer is that we can be completely open and vulnerable with God. We don't need to sugarcoat anything or clean it up for Him. He doesn't roll His eyes or sigh when we come before Him struggling again. Elijah knew this about the Lord and his is one of the most honest prayers in Scripture.

"Just let me die," Elijah prayed. He was weary and worn and, frankly, had had enough of the world. God didn't tell him to perk up, get over it, or put his big boy pants on. No, God let Elijah take a nap, then He fed him and sent him back on mission. We can share with the Lord everything we are feeling. He can handle our honest prayers.

Heavenly Father, I humbly come to You today. I may not know the words to pray, but I invite You to seek my heart and mind for all of my unspoken prayers.

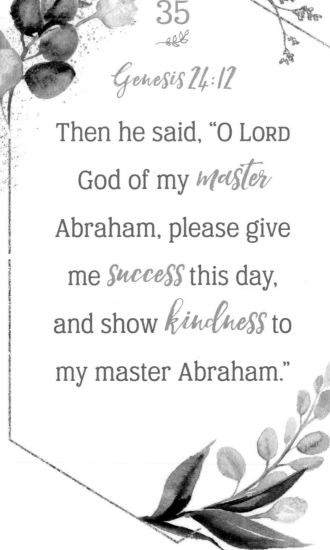

35

Genesis 24:12

Then he said, "O LORD
God of my *master*
Abraham, please give
me *success* this day,
and show *kindness* to
my master Abraham."

PRAYER FOR SUCCESS

*W*hat is the secret to success? Is it hard work, a large social media following, or just good old-fashioned stick-to-itiveness? Many have prided themselves on being "self-made" men and women. But Abraham's oldest, most faithful servant knew the secret; he prayed to the Lord to grant him success in his endeavor.

His mission was to find a wife for Abraham's son, Isaac, and the servant desperately wanted to do well by his master. So he prayed that God would be so kind as to help him succeed. And God did exactly that. He led the servant to the perfect wife for Isaac and confirmed it with the very sign the servant had asked for in advance (Genesis 24:14).

How many times have we set out to accomplish something without seeking direction from the Lord? How often do we plan and prepare, but fail to pause and pray? We make our lists but fail to enlist the help of the One "who is able to do exceedingly abundantly above" anything we could ask or think (Ephesians 3:20.)

What plans or projects do we currently have in the works? We all probably have more items than necessary on our agendas. Some of them could certainly be set aside. As for the rest, let's stop and ask the Lord to grant us success in those things that would bring Him glory.

> Thank You, Lord, for all of the many successes in
> my life. From my first breath to my last, my life is
> full of victory and triumph because of You.

36

2 Samuel 7:28

And now, O Lord God, *You*
are God, and Your words
are *true*, and You have
promised this *goodness*
to Your servant.

TRUE WORDS

*D*o you ever put pressure on yourself to make your prayer time something extravagant? Perhaps you think you must sit a certain way, use certain words, or spend a certain amount of time. We've all likely compared our time with the Lord to someone else's and felt somehow inferior.

These words of David are from later in his life and are a beautiful example of a simple yet sincere prayer. It is a reminder to us that we often make things more difficult than is necessary. In this prayer, David reminded himself of three important aspects in his relationship with God that influenced the way he prayed.

First, David prayed, "You are God." It's important to remember that we are praying to the one true God who has chosen to reveal Himself to us and to have a relationship with us.

Next, David declared that he knew the words of God to be true. He believed what Scripture said to be true of God. God cannot lie (Numbers 23:19).

Finally, David knew that God had promised goodness to him. David knew Scripture, he believed the words of the prophets, and he knew what promises God had made concerning himself and his family.

Our prayer lives would be more meaningful if we simply remind ourselves of who is hearing us. He is God. His every word is true. And He has promised us good things.

You are God, faithful and true. Make me more like You.

37

1 Kings 8:56

Blessed be the LORD, who
has given rest to His people
Israel, according to all that
He *promised*. There has
not failed one *word* of all
His *good* promise, which
He promised through
His servant Moses.

PRAYER TO THE PROMISE KEEPER

We all know at least one person that we would label as reliable. If we're ever in a bind, we call that person. Yet even the most trustworthy individual is capable of breaking his word. Illness, calendar conflicts, or any number of things could cause someone to be unable to do what he said he would do.

Solomon's prayer reminds us that this is not the case with God. He finished his prayer by reminding himself and the people that not one word of all that God had promised had failed to come to fruition. As Solomon looked back at all that God had promised to His people, he found Him faithful.

Scripture tells us that God is "the same yesterday, today, and forever" (Hebrews 13:8). He is still a keeper of His Word today, just as He was in Solomon's day. When we encounter a trial, we can thank Him in advance for His presence and His guidance because He has promised these things to His people. When we sin, we can thank Him for His forgiveness because He has promised it to those who repent and believe.

Every word that proceeds from the mouth of God proves true (Proverbs 30:5) and all of His promises are fulfilled in Christ (2 Corinthians 1:20). God is a promise keeper.

Lord, thank You for being the same yesterday,
today, and forever. Thank You for being the
Living God whom I can count on.

38

Daniel 9:18

O my God, incline Your ear
and *hear*; open Your eyes
and *see* our desolations,
and the city which is
called by Your *name*; for
we do not present our
supplications before You
because of our righteous
deeds, but because of
Your great *mercies*.

BECAUSE OF MERCY

*H*ave you ever wanted to come before the Lord with a need, but felt unworthy to even present your request to Him? It's often difficult to ask anything of Him when we know how often we fail to live according to His Word. Sometimes the very thing we seek relief from is a consequence of our own behavior.

Daniel's prayer is a great reminder of why we are able to come before God in the first place. Do you know what Daniel felt the people deserved? Shame (Daniel 9:8). Daniel confessed that they had failed to listen to the prophets God had graciously sent to them. They had openly rebelled against the Lord. Daniel referred to himself and the people as wicked.

Then he prayed for God to look upon their desolation, to hear the prayers of His people, and to make His face shine upon them (v. 17). Daniel confessed that the people deserved shame and, in the same breath, asked that God bring an end to their suffering. How could he be so bold?

Daniel knew that God's willingness to hear and to act was not based on the righteousness of those praying, but on his own abundant mercy. We come before God the same way. None of us are deserving of His intervention but, because of His great mercy, His ears are open to our cries.

God, You are my refuge. Thank You for redeeming my suffering and shame. Thank You for Your abundant mercy.

39

John 12:28

"Father,
glorify
Your
name."

YOUR NAME

*O*ur prayers are often focused on ourselves or on situations that directly affect us. This isn't wrong. After all, God instructs us to make our requests known to Him (Philippians 4:6). But what if our deepest desires and most prevalent petitions were for God to receive glory in our circumstances?

As Jesus entered this time of prayer, His very soul was troubled (John 12:27). He knew that He was nearing the time of His betrayal, which would be soon followed by His death. He asked the crowd, "What shall I say?" though it was a rhetorical question. He immediately prayed, "Father, glorify Your name."

At that moment, in the face of physical threats and emotional turmoil, Jesus prayed for God's name to be glorified. For this purpose, He was willing to suffer and die. David prayed this same sentiment in Psalm 103:1 when he said, "Bless the Lord, O my soul, and all that is within me, bless His holy name!"

> Father, help our chief desire to be for Your glory.
> May we, in every circumstance, point others to
> You. We will proclaim Your goodness so that You
> receive the honor and glory due Your name.

40

Psalm 119:132

Look upon me and
be *merciful* to me,
as Your *custom* is
toward those who
love Your name.

GOD'S CUSTOM

*H*ave you ever described someone's behavior and followed it up with, "You know how they are"? We all have people in our lives whose response to a given situation is pretty predictable. Maybe you know exactly how your mom will react to a broken lamp or that your boss will be in a bad mood if his favorite ball team loses. It can be comforting or concerning when we can anticipate someone's actions.

The writer of Psalm 119 was intimately acquainted with the ways of the Lord, and this knowledge brought him peace. He knew that it was God's way to be merciful to His people. When we consistently spend time in prayer and the study of God's Word, we can also become familiar with His custom of mercy. We know that He will never overlook sin, but we can also know that He is quick to forgive and generous with His grace.

Regardless of what we've done or where we find ourselves, those of us who have repented and believed the gospel can appeal to the Lord in this way. We can come before Him, confess our areas of disobedience, and ask that He be merciful to us, knowing that is just the way He is toward those who love Him. It's the custom of God to give mercy.

> Lord, thank You for giving me a new day, an
> opportunity for me to see people newly.

41

Psalm 90:12

So *teach* us to
number our days,
that we may *gain*
a heart of *wisdom*.

NUMBER OUR DAYS

*H*ave you ever regretted the way you have spent your time? Or mourned a missed opportunity? Wished you had been more *in the moment*? We all have been guilty of wasting time and living as if tomorrow were a guarantee.

In this prayer, Moses asked the Lord to teach him how to live with an appreciation for each day. He wanted to live with an awareness of the fragility and brevity of life. Moses' prayer is a reminder to us that man is but dust (Psalm 90:3) and that man's days "are like a dream" (v. 5 ESV).

How would we live differently if we approached each day as though it were a gift? What if we awoke each morning in awe that God had blessed us with another twenty-four hours to use for His glory? Perhaps there is an even better question: What would our lives look like if we treated each day as if it could be our last? Because let's be honest; it certainly could.

According to Moses' prayer, living with an appreciation for each day and an awareness of the fleeting nature of life would cause us to live wisely. "Teach us to number our days," Moses prayed, "*that* we may gain a heart of wisdom" (emphasis added). Let's be wise, not wasteful, with the lives God has given us.

> Father, give me the wisdom and the courage
> to use my time as You see worthy.

42

Psalm 61:1-2

Hear my cry, O God;
attend to my *prayer*. From
the end of the earth I
will cry to You, when my
heart is overwhelmed;
lead me to the rock
that is *higher* than I.

HIGHER THAN I

*W*hen is the last time you felt overwhelmed? Most of us have probably experienced it in the last week, if not the last twenty-four hours. Jesus warned us that there will certainly be trials and tribulations that come our way. So what are we to do during those times?

There are numerous ways the world encourages us to respond in overwhelming situations. We may want to attempt to hide from everyone and everything around us. Or we might become envious of others who seem to be having an easier time. Perhaps we will be tempted to become bitter.

David knew the best way to handle deeply distressing circumstances. He prayed and cried out to God. David's prayer holds a precious reminder to us that we are never too far away for God to hear us. "From the end of the earth . . . ," David said. He trusted that the Lord could hear his cries and could tend to whatever trouble he had encountered.

Lord, we will not turn away from You in times of trial. We will cry out to You and trust You to work on our behalf. We are never too far away for our cries to reach You ears. Hear us, O Lord, answer our pleas, and lead us to You.

43

Psalm 23:1

The *Lord* is my *shepherd*; I shall not want.

I SHALL NOT WANT

*H*ave you ever known a portion of Scripture so well that you could recite it without even thinking? For anyone who has spent a large amount of time in church or reading Scripture, Psalm 23 is probably one of those passages. But it becomes easy to skim the words and miss the wonder.

David believed that he lacked nothing as long as the Lord was his shepherd. He experienced what the children of Israel experienced on their journey through the wilderness. The Lord journeyed with them for forty years, and they "lacked nothing" (Deuteronomy 2:7). God is who He has always been.

God also journeys with us through our personal wildernesses, whatever that may look like. It may be physical pain, financial strain, broken relationships, or broken dreams. Whatever the situation, the Lord knows how long we've been wandering and enduring. And we can know that when we follow Him we will have everything we need.

God was aware of every step the children of Israel took. He saw every struggle, heard every cry, and they lacked nothing. The same is true for us today. Jesus taught that we don't need to worry because God is aware of what we need (Matthew 6:8), and He is willing and able to provide. The Lord is still our shepherd and, with Him, we shall not want.

> Teach me, Lord, to want those things
> that are most pleasing to You.

44

Psalm 85:6

Will You not *revive*
us again, that
Your people may
rejoice in You?

PRAYER FOR REVIVAL

*T*he world seems to be moving faster each day, and we're all struggling to keep up. We feel the need to accomplish and acquire more, and—let's be honest—it's exhausting. We exert energy on things that don't satisfy. Our devotion is directed in all the wrong places, causing our spirits to run down.

The prayer found in Psalm 85 contains the pleas of an entire community who were suffering the consequences of taking their focus off God. Their spirits were drained, and they were desperate for revival. In their prayer, we see three important elements of the restoration the people desired.

One, only God could revive them. No larger achievement or greater popularity could grant them what their spirits needed. Only the One who had initially breathed life into them could breathe fresh life into them.

Second, they trusted God to revive them *again.* The children of Israel made the very same mistakes time and again. Can't we all relate to trying again the very thing that didn't work for us before? Or doing the thing we swore we weren't going to do again?

Finally, they knew that revival would result in joy. It took humility to come before God and ask for revival when it was sin that had left them run down and weary. But they were confident in the joy that was to come. They were confident in the power of God to revive them.

> Everlasting Father, I come to You for revival. I ask that You restore my joy and vitality for Your glory.

45

Proverbs 30:7–9

Two things I *request* of You
(deprive me not before I die):
Remove falsehood and lies
far from me; *give* me neither
poverty nor riches—*feed* me
with the food allotted to me;
lest I be *full* and deny You,
and say, "Who is the *Lord*?" Or
lest I be poor and steal, and
profane the name of my God.

AN HONEST, SIMPLE LIFE

Sometimes our prayers can become complicated. We tend to outline everything we think we need to make our lives more fulfilling, comfortable, or meaningful. There are certainly seasons when our needs are great and our prayers reflect the overwhelming nature of our circumstances. But there are many times when this simple prayer from Proverbs would suffice.

This prayer is uttered by a man who was admittedly weary and worn out. He confessed that he had not learned the things he should have learned by this point in his life (Proverbs 30:3). Life had become too much for him, and in this prayer, he reminded himself of the all-powerful and trustworthy nature of God. After pondering these aspects of God, he then made his request of the Lord.

So what does a weary and worn-out man desire from God? First, he asked God to help him live an *honest* life. He wanted any areas of falsehood or deception to be removed far from him. Second, he requested that the Lord help him to live a *simple* life. He trusted God to give him neither too much nor too little, but exactly what he needed.

Doesn't that sound wonderful? Let's seek to live honestly in our words, actions, and dealings with others. And then let's seek ways to simplify our possessions, calendars, and activities. There is beauty in an honest and simple life.

Lord, lead me down the path to living an honest and simple life. Teach me how to be fulfilled by You alone.

46

Psalm 25:4–5

Show me Your ways,
O Lord; *teach* me Your
paths. *Lead* me in Your
truth and teach me,
for You are the God of
my *salvation*; on You
I wait all the day.

YOUR WAYS

*E*veryone has their own way of doing things. We each have our own way of relaxing, traveling, and organizing our homes. We take our coffee various ways and have different routines. And if someone has ever folded your bath towels the wrong way, you know that we can be pretty committed to the way we do things.

David was certainly no different. He was a skilled shepherd, mighty musician, and conquering king. There had to be areas in which he preferred to have things done a certain way with no room for discussion. Knowing this, his prayer showed true humility on David's part as he asked, "Show me Your ways, O LORD."

Just like today, people mentioned in Scripture were faced with a world full of people who did things contrary to what the Lord commanded. David genuinely desired to live a life centered around the things of God. He asked the Lord to reveal His ways, paths, and truth. Why? Because he knew that God was the source of his salvation.

What if we all approached life this way? What would it look like for us, in every scenario, to ask God to reveal to us His way of doing things?

> Lord, give us humble hearts that desire
> Your way in all aspects of our lives.

47

Ephesians 3:17-19

That you, being *rooted* and grounded in love, may be able to comprehend with all the *saints* what is the width and length and depth and height— to know the *love* of Christ which passes knowledge; that you may be filled with all the *fullness* of God.

LOVE OF CHRIST

The word "love" has become so misused and overused in our culture. We love our spouses, our coffee, or a good book, and it's often difficult to differentiate our feelings toward various things. It's no wonder that it's sometimes hard to comprehend the love of Christ for us or to explain His love to someone else.

Paul's prayer was that the people who made up the church at Ephesus would truly grasp the magnitude of Christ's love. When people know how much they are loved, it changes the way they view themselves, others, and the world around them. On the other hand, a person who doesn't believe they are loved will also make decisions based on that belief.

The writer of Psalm 106 described the spiral that occurs when people forget that they are loved. The author said that they became ungrateful, disobedient, and enslaved. And it all began when they forgot about the abundance and faithfulness of God's love (v. 7).

Paul's prayer for the Ephesians is a reminder to us that we need to pray for those around us. When we don't understand someone's behavior or why they make the choices they make, it may just be that they don't grasp the width, length, depth, and height of Christ's love for them.

> Father, show me how to love others
> unconditionally and abundantly.

48

Jeremiah 12:3

But You, O Lord, *know* me; You have seen me, and You have *tested* my *heart* toward You.

THE GOD WHO SEES

Sometimes when my children fall down, I pretend I don't notice. Please don't judge me. I've come to realize that if they think I didn't see, they often carry on with whatever they were doing prior to the fall. If I make eye contact, however, weeping and wailing may commence. It's just a little parenting hack I've found helpful.

Aren't we glad that God doesn't do that with us? He doesn't look away from the broken, the weak, or the fallen. He saw Hagar sitting by a spring in the wilderness (Genesis 16:7), and Jeremiah knew that God saw him as well. Understanding that God is *El Roi*—the God who sees—made a huge impact in their lives. The need to know that God sees us is not new.

Jesus conducted His earthly ministry the same way. Jesus never looked away, neither from the leper nor the lame, the Pharisee or the prostitute. Not from you or me in our time of need. And those of us who call ourselves Christ followers must love the same way.

People who are hurting don't need us to avoid eye contact or pretend not to notice their pain. We don't look away when it's inconvenient or uncomfortable. Sometimes, the greatest act of love toward someone can be to simply see them. Let's look someone in the eye today and make them feel seen.

Open the eyes of my heart, Lord, so that I
can see others the way You see them.

49

Jonah 4:2

So he *prayed* to the LORD, and
said, "Ah, LORD, was not this
what I said when I was still
in my *country*? Therefore I
fled previously to Tarshish;
for I know that You are a
gracious and merciful God,
slow to anger and *abundant*
in lovingkindness, One who
relents from doing harm."

PRAYER OF CONFESSION

This may be one of the most honest prayers in Scripture. It would be almost comical, in fact, if Jonah had not been so sincerely distraught over the whole situation. He was told to go to the people of Nineveh and call them to repentance—a common mission and message in Scripture, but Jonah outright disobeyed and fled in the opposite direction.

However, Jonah gets back on track and heads to his destination. He preaches to the people and all of them, from the greatest to the least, repent and believe (Jonah 3:5). One would think that Jonah would be thrilled with such a response to his message, but that was not the case at all.

Jonah was "exceedingly" displeased and "angry." It is at this point that he utters his extremely honest prayer. In the language of today, his words would read something like this: "That is why I didn't want to go, Lord. I knew You would save them because that is the way You operate." Jonah knew that the Lord was gracious and merciful, and he didn't believe the people in Nineveh deserved those things.

Is there someone in our lives that we view as too far gone? Unworthy of the mercy and grace of God? Let's confess and repent of those thoughts and then ask God to soften our hearts toward those individuals.

Father, I choose to confess and repent of the thoughts I've held that keep me separate from others, and ultimately from You. I ask that You cleanse my thoughts and renew my mind.

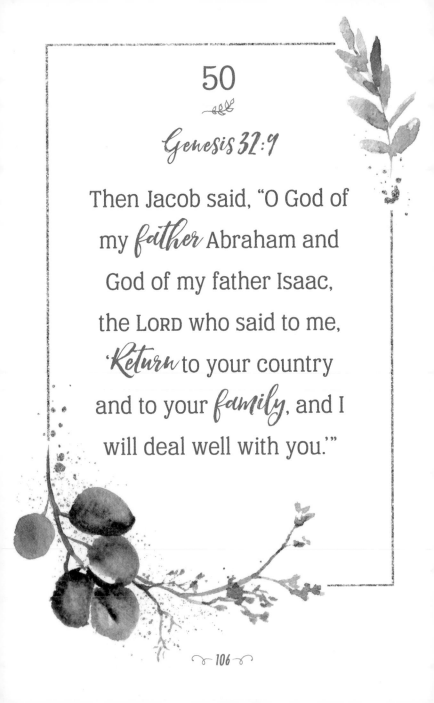

50

Genesis 32:9

Then Jacob said, "O God of
my *father* Abraham and
God of my father Isaac,
the Lord who said to me,
'*Return* to your country
and to your *family*, and I
will deal well with you.'"

PRAYER TO OVERCOME FEAR

There are things in this world that cause little seeds of fear to plant themselves deep in our hearts. We may fear earthly disasters or health issues. Maybe we fear darkness, dogs, or heights. Imagine, for a moment, that God instructs you to confront the very thing you fear the most.

God sent Jacob back to face the brother he had betrayed many years before. Scripture tells us that Jacob was "greatly afraid and distressed" (Genesis 32:7). His response was to pray and, in his prayer, we can learn how to respond when facing our own fears.

First, Jacob turned to God. We see that immediately upon receiving this direction from God, he prayed. Then Jacob acknowledged his place before God (v. 10). He knew that he was not worthy for God to intervene because it was his own sin that had caused a rift in his relationship with his brother.

The next thing Jacob did was to simply confess his fear to the Lord (v. 11). What if we didn't play the "I'm okay" game with God? After all, He knows the truth. We don't have to pretend with Him. Finally, Jacob knew the promises God had made (v. 12) and that He could be trusted to keep them. Let's learn from Jacob's example and begin taking the steps to overcome our own fears by turning to God in prayer.

Heavenly Father, I ask for faith and
courage to face my fears.

51

Ephesians 3:20-21

Now to *Him* who is able to do exceedingly abundantly above all that we ask or think, according to the *power* that works in us, to Him be *glory* in the church by Christ Jesus to all generations, *forever* and ever. Amen.

ABOVE AND BEYOND

Most of us, without realizing it, are probably guilty of praying weak prayers. We ask an all-powerful, omniscient, omnipresent God to do what *we* think is possible or reasonable in a given situation. A doctor tells us there's no hope, and so we pray for comfort for our loved one when what we truly desire is complete healing.

Paul knew he was praying to the One who was capable of doing far more than the people could even think to ask. "Exceedingly abundantly above," Paul said. And so he ended this prayer in Ephesians with a reminder of the power of God.

Is there a situation in your life that seems hopeless? Do you have a prodigal that others consider a lost cause? What is that thing you long for but gave up on long ago? Through Christ, we are given permission to boldly approach the throne (Hebrews 4:16).

How would it change our prayers if we were bold with our requests? What would we ask of God if we truly believed *anything* was possible? We serve a God who is capable of exceedingly abundantly more than we can even think or imagine. May our prayers reflect this powerful truth.

Lord, with You anything is possible. Help me
to see where I am playing it safe. Teach me to
play full-out knowing You are on my side.

52

2 Kings 6:18

So when the Syrians came down to him, Elisha *prayed* to the LORD, and said, "*Strike* this people, I *pray*, with blindness." And He struck them with blindness according to the *word* of Elisha.

PRAYER AGAINST AN ENEMY

*W*e have an Enemy who desires to do us harm. We may get caught up in all the busyness of life and become distracted, but we can be certain that Satan does not forget. He is scheming and seeking ways to destroy God's people. With this in mind, when we come before the Lord in prayer, how often do we pray for protection from our Enemy?

Elisha was aware that the Syrian army was close at hand, and he wasn't shy about seeking the Lord's intervention against this enemy. "Strike them blind," he prayed. He knew he couldn't defeat the enemy on his own, but he also knew that the Lord was greater than the enemy. God responded by striking the Syrians blind just as Elisha had asked.

We tend to minimize the very real and present reality of our greatest Enemy. We have turned Satan into a caricature and, by doing so, made him less scary. We've made him so unassuming, in fact, that we often think we can handle him on our own. With this mindset, Satan has us exactly where he wants us.

Let's make it a regular habit to pray for our protection against the Enemy. Just as the Syrians were real for Elisha, Satan is very real for us. He is near to us (Romans 7:21), and we can't defeat him on our own. But greater is He who is in us than he who is in the world (1 John 4:4).

Lord, I ask for Your protection against the Enemy. Protect my mind and my heart, and help keep my path straight.

53

Philippians 1:9-10

And this I pray, that your *love* may abound still more and more in *knowledge* and all *discernment*, that you may approve the things that are *excellent*, that you may be *sincere* and without offense till the day of *Christ*.

PRAYER FOR DISCERNMENT

*I*f you've ever enjoyed an old western show on television, you know that there was never any confusion as to who was the *good guy* and who was the *bad guy*. The good guy usually wore the badge, while the music turned eerie when the villain came on the scene. There were multiple cues to alert us to everyone's role.

This is not the case in the real world. As much as we may think it's a modern problem, the line between good and evil was blurry in Paul's day as well. When praying for the Philippian church, Paul asked that they would have discernment and the ability to choose what was excellent.

The reality is that the enemy doesn't always present himself as blatantly evil. He doesn't show up wearing the black hat and twisting his handlebar mustache. Instead, we often find ourselves having to choose between what is good and what is best. Or we attempt to convince ourselves that something is "not *that* bad." And then there are those times when we simply don't know which choice is the correct one.

It takes true discernment to live a godly life. We must, as Paul prayed, be able to choose the things that are excellent.

Help us, Lord, to meditate on Your Word so
that Your ways are obvious to us.

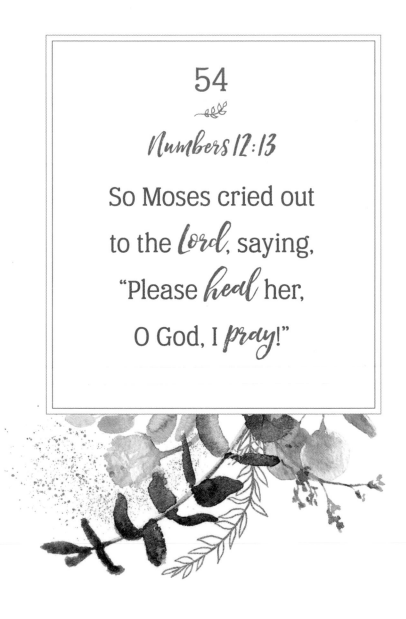

54

Numbers 12:13

So Moses cried out
to the *Lord*, saying,
"Please *heal* her,
O God, I *pray*!"

PRAYER FOR HEALING

*M*iriam had dared to speak ill of Moses. But Moses was not only her brother, he was a prophet of the Lord. God took this offense so seriously that He caused Miriam to be covered in leprosy. It certainly wasn't always the case, but in this instance her illness was a direct result of her sinful actions.

Moses' immediate reaction was to cry out to God on her behalf. He prayed that Miriam would be healed of her affliction Moses expressed such humility in not only forgiving the original offense, but also pleading for the consequences of that offense to be removed from her.

How many of us have seen another individual dealing with the unpleasant ramifications of his or her behavior and failed to feel any compassion? Perhaps we thought to ourselves, "Well, that's what he gets," or some such sentiment. Maybe we even fail to pray for our own healing because we feel that we deserve whatever it is that has happened to us.

There are two things that make all the difference when it comes to a seemingly undeserved healing. First, God is a merciful God, and His mercies are new every morning (Lamentations 3:23). Second, prayer is a powerful thing. The prayer of a righteous man can accomplish much good (James 5:16). Let's pray for the healing of those around us.

God of mercy, I pray for those around me, that they would know Your peace, healing, and love.

55

John 17:9

"I *pray* for them.
I do not pray for
the *world* but
for those whom
You have given
Me, for they
are *Yours.*"

JESUS PRAYS FOR US

*W*ho do you want praying for you when you encounter a trial? Hopefully, we all have someone who we know will spend time pleading with the Lord on our behalf. What is it about a specific individual that makes us trust them with our deepest desires or secret struggles?

Jesus' prayer life is heavily documented in Scripture, and it serves to teach us of the extreme importance of the spiritual discipline. This particular prayer by Jesus gives three key elements that are essential to look for in a potential prayer partner. These are also the three things that should be evident in our own prayer lives as we intercede for others.

First, Jesus literally prayed. It seems obvious, but how many of us have said we would pray about something and never actually did? We have the best of intentions, and then fail to follow through. Jesus prayed often.

Second, Jesus prayed for us specifically. It wasn't a general, bless-the-whole-world kind of prayer. Jesus withdrew to a desolate place and prayed for us. Don't we want someone calling us by name before the Father?

Finally, Jesus acknowledged that we belonged to God. He knew our value. How would it change our prayers for others if we looked at them as precious to their heavenly Father? Let's take the time to pray for others, to pray for them by name, and to remember their value to God.

Thank You, Lord, for praying on my behalf, and for bridging the gap where I fall short of the glory of God.

56

Judges 13:8

Then Manoah *prayed* to the LORD, and said, "O my Lord, *please* let the Man of God whom You sent come to us again and *teach* us what we shall do for the *child* who will be born."

PRAYER FOR PARENTING

*M*anoah's wife was barren, but as is always the case with the Lord, her medical condition couldn't stop His miracle from coming. An angel of the Lord came to this woman and, after confirming that she was in fact barren and had never borne a child, declared that she was about to conceive a son (Judges 13:2–3). The woman relayed the message to Manoah and his response is the heart's cry of every parent: "Can you teach us what we should do for the child?"

Every parent knows the initial feeling of fear and shock when someone hands you a seven-pound miracle and then just lets you walk away with it. There are so many things to learn when you're a new parent. But Manoah's concern wasn't related to late-night feedings or sleep schedules.

This new father prayed that God would teach him how to prepare his child to fulfill his purpose in life. He wanted to know what the child's mission would be (v. 12) and what he could do to properly train him for it. Imagine if we all prayed that over our children.

Father, teach us how to raise children who live
out Your purpose for their lives. May they be
filled with Your Spirit and on fire for Your glory.
Help us equip them for kingdom work.

57

2 Kings 20:3

Remember now, O LORD, I pray, how I have *walked* before You in *truth* and with a *loyal* heart, and have done what was *good* in Your sight.

THE POWER OF PRAYER

*H*ave you ever been tempted to not pray over some-thing? Perhaps the outcome seemed predetermined or a positive resolution too unlikely. Maybe we wouldn't verbalize it as such, but our lack of prayer over a matter indicates that we doubt God's ability or willingness to act on our behalf. Prayer may just be the least utilized weapon by God's people.

Hezekiah knew the power of prayer, and he understood that things happen in unseen places when God's people call on His name. Through the prophet, Isaiah, the Lord Himself sent Hezekiah a message: "Set your house in order," the Lord said, "for you shall die" (2 Kings 20:1). Hezekiah didn't just accept his death; he prayed and asked the Lord to remember the righteous way he had lived. And God heard.

In response to Hezekiah's prayer, the Lord sent another message through Isaiah. This time the news was much more favorable. "I've heard your prayer," the Lord said, and he granted Hezekiah fifteen more years of life (v. 6). Fifteen years of festivals, family, and faithful living were granted to him.

What do we not have because we have not asked for it? Our prayers would be radically different if we truly believed that anything was possible.

Lord, teach us the unlimited power of prayer.

58

Job 32:21

Let me not, I
pray, show
partiality to anyone;
nor let me
flatter
any man.

PRAYER FOR GODLY RELATIONSHIPS

It's really difficult to not show partiality to anyone. We tend to judge people based on who they know, what they do, or how they look, and then act accordingly. But that is the world's way of interacting with and evaluating people. It's not God's way.

Scripture is clear that man looks on the outward parts of a man, but God looks on the heart (1Samuel 16:7). We can easily be deceived regarding someone's character if we make assumptions based on where they live or what they drive. The things they say and the way they treat people, however, reveals what is in their hearts.

Job's prayer highlighted two aspects of godly relationships. First, godly relationships are genuine. We care about someone as an individual. We don't choose our friends because of what they can do for us, nor do we reject someone because of what others may say.

Second, godly relationships are honest. Flattery feels good for a moment, but an honest friend can be trusted for a lifetime. Real relationships have openness, vulnerability, and accountability.

Lord, help us to develop godly relationships
that are genuine and honest.

59

Psalm 17:15

As for *me*, I will
see Your face in
righteousness; I
shall be satisfied
when I *awake* in
Your likeness.

PRAYER OF SATISFACTION

*A*s followers of Christ, we often look around and feel like we simply don't fit in with the world in which we live. Our desires, our view of the world, and our understanding of what truly matters is drastically different from those who don't know the Lord. This was also the case in David's day.

In this prayer, David outlined some of the behaviors of the wicked men with whom he was dealing. He was being oppressed, harassed, and surrounded. David described them as having closed hearts and proud lips (Psalm 17:10).

The biggest difference was what brought them ultimate satisfaction. The wicked received all of their rewards in this life. They were satisfied, David said, with their children and their possessions. It was not so for David. "As for me," he prayed, "I will be satisfied with seeing Your likeness" (NIV).

This world parades a lot of pretty things before our eyes. It offers plenty of shiny distractions meant to mimic fulfillment and satisfaction. Just like in David's day, people take pride in their families, possessions, and achievements. Let our prayer be the same as the man after God's own heart.

> Only You, Lord, can satisfy the longings
> of our hearts, and we will not know true
> satisfaction until we are in Your presence.

60

John 17:15

"I do not pray that *You* should take them out of the *world*, but that You should *keep* them from the evil one."

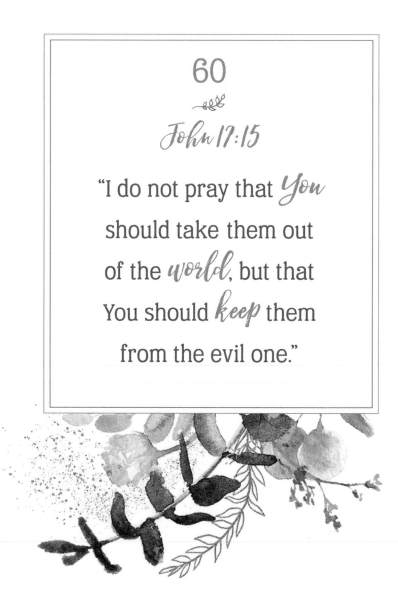

PRAYER FOR PROTECTION

*W*ho among us enjoys being uncomfortable? Persecuted? Afflicted? It's a silly question, of course. Were we given the option, we would all choose a life of coffee drinking and front porch sitting. Or as believers, we would opt for the fast-pass to heaven.

As Jesus prayed for His disciples, He knew all that the future held for them. He knew they were going to face beatings, imprisonments, and rejection. However, Jesus didn't ask the Father to prevent all the pain and take them home. He clearly told Peter that while they would be with Him soon, they couldn't join Him in heaven yet (John 13:36). There was still work to be done on earth, and people (you and me, for example) would come to faith because of the disciples' testimonies (17:20).

Jesus didn't pray for the pain of the disciples to be prevented. He prayed for their protection in the midst of it. Let's make that our prayer as well—for ourselves, our children, and fellow believers.

We have been placed in this world at a specific point in time, in a particular geographic location, and with a unique set of gifts and talents.

Help us, Lord, to fight the good fight and to keep the faith. Protect us from the schemes of the Enemy so that we are not distracted from our kingdom purposes.

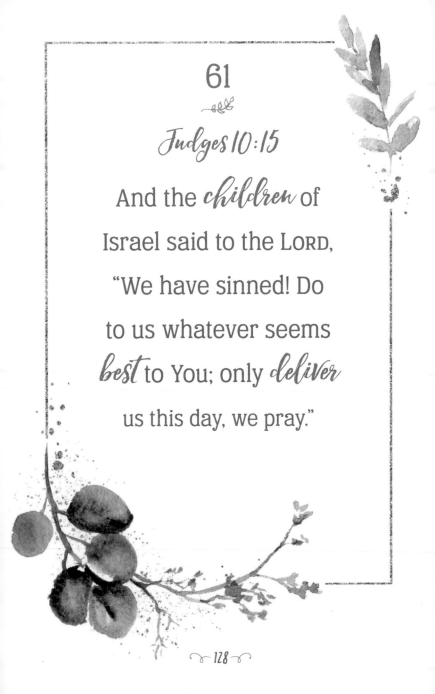

61

Judges 10:15

And the *children* of
Israel said to the Lord,
"We have sinned! Do
to us whatever seems
best to You; only *deliver*
us this day, we pray."

PRAYER OF TRUST

We place a lot of trust in a variety of people and things. We sit in a chair and trust that it will hold our weight. Sometimes we trust people to drive or fly us where we need to go. In times of illness, we trust that our doctors know the best way to care for us.

But how many of us, after hurting or wronging someone, would trust them enough to say, "Do whatever seems best to you"? Or after admitting that we have wronged someone, ask for their immediate assistance? It's almost comical.

Yet this is exactly what the children of Israel did. They prayed that the Lord would do whatever seemed best to Him in response to their sin. They trusted His response to be just and in line with His character.

David had a similar response when he sinned against the Lord and was given the choice of punishments. "Let us fall into the Lord's hands because his mercies are great, but don't let me fall into human hands," (2 Samuel 24:14 csb). He trusted the character of God.

Lord, when we disobey and lose our way, we trust Your correction and discipline. Do whatever seems best to You.

62

Psalm 32:7

You are my hiding place; You shall *preserve* me from trouble; You shall *surround* me with *songs* of deliverance.

PRAYER OF PRESERVATION

*W*e all have a place where we go in times of trouble. It might be a storm shelter in instances of literal storms, or it may be a certain place or person to help us when we experience inner turmoil. As children, we probably all tried the "If I can't see you then you can't see me" trick as we hid under our covers from any potential boogeymen.

When seeking shelter from turmoil and trials, David knew to whom he could turn. The Lord was his safe place in any storm, and he trusted in His ability and willingness to preserve his life in the face of danger. Protection, preservation, and victory were his in the presence of God.

Everyone is going to encounter troubles in this life. No one makes it through unscathed. In seasons of struggle, the difference between those who belong to God and those who reject Him is where they turn. The world offers temporary reprieves from pain, but only God provides victory.

As God's children, we all have a safe place to which we can run. When we need a moment of peace, the Lord will cover us with His wings (Psalm 91:4). When trouble arises, He will preserve our coming and our going (121:8). Then, when our work on earth is done, He will deliver us safely home.

Lord, cover us with Your wings of protection
and deliver us safely home to You.

63

Psalm 51:1

Have *mercy* upon me,
O God, according to
Your *lovingkindness*;
according to the
multitude of Your
tender mercies, blot out
my transgressions.

PRAYER FOR RESTORATION

*H*ave you ever had a friendship that was fractured because one person betrayed, let down, or somehow offended the other? Even when apologies had been made and forgiveness offered, the relationship was probably never quite the same. There's often an awkwardness or lack of trust that permanently mars any interactions between the parties involved.

David messed up in a major way when he sinned with Bathsheba. The Lord called him out and the consequences for his behavior were great. David was aware of the egregious nature of his actions (Psalm 51:3), and he desperately desired to be cleansed. But his immediate request of the Lord was for restoration.

David prayed that God would blot out his transgressions. The Hebrew word that David used was *machah*. This wasn't a plea to avoid punishment for there would be no getting out of that. This idea of blotting out was more along the lines of wiping the slate clean. "Could we," David was essentially asking, "be as we were before? As if this never happened?"

When we repent and return to God, He is faithful and just to forgive us (1 John 1:9). His forgiveness is complete and the slate is wiped clean. We may still deal with consequences related to our behavior, but God will never hold our failing against us. His mercy is abundant.

Only You, Father, can blot out our transgressions.
Thank You for Your abundance of love and mercy.

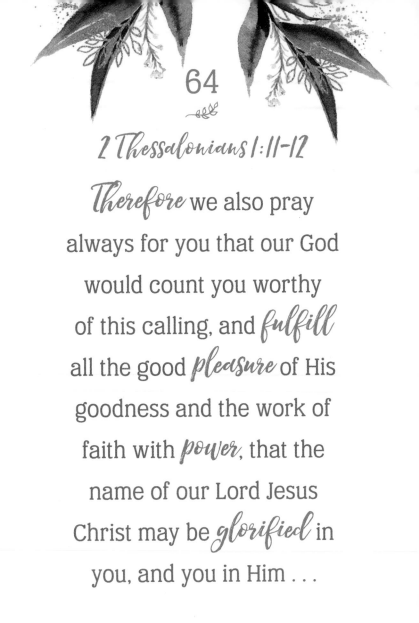

64

2 Thessalonians 1:11–12

Therefore we also pray always for you that our God would count you worthy of this calling, and *fulfill* all the good *pleasure* of His goodness and the work of faith with *power*, that the name of our Lord Jesus Christ may be *glorified* in you, and you in Him . . .

GLORIFIED IN US

*I*t's tempting to live in such a way as to make a name for ourselves. We want to be known and, perhaps, to achieve some level of greatness. Praise and applause can become addicting and cause our priorities in life to shift. But none of us have been created to bring glory to ourselves.

Paul's prayer for the Thessalonian believers was that *the name of the Lord* would be glorified in them. He desired that they would live in such a way as to be counted worthy of God's calling on their lives, and it was a calling that included suffering (2 Thessalonians 1:5). Paul prayed that the Lord would make the people worthy, help them remain committed to doing good, and to keep the faith. But the end aim of it all was that God would receive the glory.

Who receives the glory in our lives? If someone were to evaluate the way we spend our time, energy, and money, what would it say about us? Are we committed to doing good, or only when it's convenient? Do we have a faith that is firm in the face of suffering, or does it prove to be fickle?

Lord, help us to live worthy of the calling You have placed within us. May others look at us, see our good works, and give You the glory for it all.

65

Colossians 4:3

Meanwhile *praying*
also for us, that God
would *open* to us a
door for the word,
to speak the *mystery*
of Christ, for which I
am also in chains.

PRAYER FOR AN OPEN DOOR

The most experienced evangelist probably feels a little nervous when sharing the gospel with another person because of the great importance of the message. For a lot of us, however, our nervousness is mostly self-focused. We worry that someone may be offended by what we say. Or perhaps we think we may not have all of the answers to their questions. Frankly, we often just don't want to inconvenience ourselves or risk looking foolish.

While in prison, Paul wrote to the Colossian church and asked the believers to pray that God would open a door for him to share the gospel. The gospel was the reason he was in chains, and yet he prayed for more opportunities to share its message. Paul was risking far more than looking foolish; he was risking his life. And he did so gladly.

How often do we begin our days by praying that God would open a door for us to speak the mystery of Christ? Would we take an opportunity to share the gospel knowing that it may result in persecution of some kind? Paul didn't view his suffering as an indication he should stop preaching; rather, he determined to preach all the more!

Fill us with the same passion, Lord. Open doors for Your Word and give us the boldness to walk through them.

66

Psalm 3:2-3

Many are they who say of me, "There is no *help* for him in God." But You, O LORD, are a *shield* for me, my glory and the One who *lifts* up my head.

BUT YOU, O LORD

There are so many voices calling out to us these days, spewing their opinions on television and filling books with their versions of truth. They are charismatic, and their words have just enough veracity to be convincing to many people. And their voices are often so very loud.

David was experiencing the overwhelming noise of the crowd when he prayed the words of Psalm 3. His foes were numerous. There were many rising up against him, and there were many who were attempting to steal his hope. It would seem that he was grossly outnumbered. But David knew something that all his enemies didn't: God always outweighs the many.

We must listen to the Master and not the multitude. He is the majority in any situation, and His voice is the only one that matters. They may have said that there was no hope for David, but their opinion didn't matter. God had already promised hope and provided comfort.

Help us, Father, to filter out the voices of the world
that attempt to instill anxiety and steal our hope.
Give us wisdom to discern what is of You and what
is of the world. We will listen for Your voice, knowing
that Your truth is all that matters in our lives.

67

~eee~

Psalm 16:11

You will show me the
path of life; in Your
presence is fullness of *joy*;
at Your right hand are
pleasures forevermore.

FULLNESS OF JOY

*W*hat would complete joy look like in your life? It's probably more than most of us could comprehend. We don't have much to compare it to in this world. The earthly version of joy is temporary and dependent upon so many outside factors.

The thing about the kind of joy David mentioned in this prayer was that it wasn't connected to an earthly place, a possession, or an achievement. David was familiar with extravagant living, man's praise, and beautiful women—and none of it was enough. He knew that true, complete, full joy was found only in the presence of God.

David believed in a day that would include perfect joy and pleasures forevermore because he would finally be in God's presence. We have access to this joy because we have access to the presence of God through faith in Jesus Christ. We too can experience the fullness of joy that David described.

We long to be with You, Father. We look forward to the day when we bask in the joy described in David's prayer. Reveal to us Your path of life, and help us remain faithful to it until the day You call us home.

68

Psalm 18:39

For You have
armed me with
strength for the battle;
You have *subdued*
under me those
who *rose* up
against me.

PRAYER FOR BATTLE

*W*hether it be with a child, a neighbor, or a coworker, we've all had to choose our battles at some point. We've had to stop and consider whether or not the situation warranted our intervention, or if the possible fallout was worth the bother. Sometimes we choose to engage, and other times we walk away.

There are times when we sense God telling us to be still. Or He may tell us to turn the other cheek and overlook an offense. Sometimes we have to stand down and let the Lord do what only He can do. This doesn't mean, however, that Christians are to be weak and never ready for battle.

David was a king who had spent a lot of time in battle. He knew the importance of fighting when it was time to fight. In this prayer, he acknowledged that it was God who had given him strength to fight that battle, but he didn't fight alone. David also knew that it was, ultimately, the Lord who successfully subdued the enemy.

Every battle is not ours to fight (2 Chronicles 20:15). We do, at times, need to walk away, even if it means our pride may be a little wounded. On the other hand, there are times when God instructs us to stand up against the Enemy and brace for battle. In those moments, the Lord trains our hands for war and our fingers for battle (Psalm 144:1).

Lord, show us when it's time to walk away,
when to be still, and when to brace for battle
in order to stand up against the Enemy.

69

Psalm 104:6-7

You *covered* it with the *deep* as with a garment; the *waters* stood above the *mountains*. At Your rebuke they fled; at the *voice* of Your *thunder* they hastened away.

IN HIS HANDS

*I*f you have ever experienced a flood or even driven through the aftermath of one, you are aware of the massive destruction that occurs after such an event. One flood that took place in Europe in 1362 was referred to as the "Great Drowning of Men" due to the tremendous loss of life. A natural disaster seems to highlight just how little control we have over our own lives.

The author of the prayer found in Psalm 104 highlighted the powerful nature of God by focusing on His control over His creation. He detailed the way God stretched out the heavens, set the earth on its foundations, and created boundaries for the bodies of water. What does this mean for us?

Most of us would readily proclaim that God is the creator of all that has been made. But we often live as if we've forgotten that He is also in control of it. We watch the news and panic over crime, politics, and global warming. This prayer is a reminder to us all that the world is not random.

God created the world with attention to every detail. He cares for animals that we don't even know exist, and He knows every star by name. Regardless of what any headline says, the sky is not falling and He still has the whole world in His hands.

> Teach me, Lord, to give up my perceived
> control and put my trust in You.

70

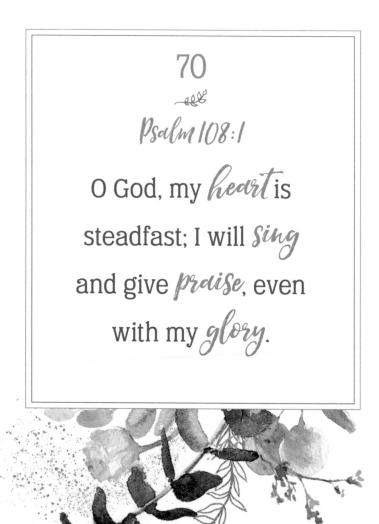

Psalm 108:1

O God, my *heart* is
steadfast; I will *sing*
and give *praise*, even
with my *glory*.

STEADFAST HEART

Prone to wander," the old hymn says. "Lord, I feel it. Prone to leave the God I love." Have you ever felt that way? Like the world was trying with all its might to pull you away from the Lord? Maybe you've been fighting the same battle for years and have grown weary. Perhaps you've prayed the same prayer and haven't yet seen it resolved the way you had hoped. Have you ever felt prone to wander?

David found himself in yet another dangerous situation involving another battle with another enemy. It was a second-verse-same-as-the-first scenario. Don't you know that David was growing a little tired of it all? I can't help but wonder if he longed for the peaceful days of living among the sheep as an unknown shepherd boy. Often, it's only in hindsight that we recognize the blessings what we had.

In this midst of his latest trial, however, David prayed this prayer. In the very first line, we see two important aspects of praying in the midst of difficult times. First, we see that David refused to stray from God's commands. Second, he believed that the Lord would deliver him, and he anticipated a time of singing and praise.

Whatever my days may hold, Father, I hold onto Your
Word tightly and maintain a steadfast heart. I am
reminded ourselves of Your promies and look forward
to a time of celebration when the battle is won.

71

Luke 22:32

"But I have *prayed* for
you, that your *faith*
should not fail; and when
you have returned to Me,
strengthen your brethren."

STRENGTHEN YOUR BRETHREN

Whose testimony has made the most difference in your life? Perhaps it was someone who had failed in some way, but persevered. Or maybe it was a person who endured a tragedy without losing their faith. Possibly it was simply a person who continually exhibited the fruit of the Spirit.

Jesus' prayer for Peter is one of the most personal, intimate prayers in Scripture. He knew the humiliating failure that Peter was about to experience, and so He prayed specifically for him. (Jesus also prays for us, by the way [Romans 8:34].)

There were three important elements to this prayer. One, Jesus prayed that Peter's faith wouldn't fail. Two, He knew that Peter would return to Him. And finally, Jesus wanted Peter to use what he had endured to strengthen his fellow believers. This meant that Peter's testimony had to be told. Aren't we glad that the stories of godly men and women are preserved in Scripture?

Lord, I gain strength from stories of the godly men and women who witnessed Your power, love, and mercy firsthand. May I also be bold enough to tell my testimony so that others may know of the hope they can have in You.

72

Psalm 130:3 ESV

If *You*, O LORD,
should mark
iniquities, O Lord,
who could
stand?

WHO COULD STAND?

*W*e are all guilty of sometimes minimizing our own sin while highlighting the failings of others. Or creating our own hierarchy of sin where one is more offensive than another. It's often difficult for us to even recognize and admit that we have sin in our own lives.

The reality, however, is found in the words of this prayer. The writer of Psalm 130 asked a rhetorical question: *If God kept an account of our sins and stumbles, who among us would be able to stand in His presence?* The answer, obviously, is that no one would be able to do it.

There are two beautiful reminders hidden in this seemingly simple prayer. First, the question is entirely hypothetical because God does not keep a record of wrongs (103:12). God's forgiveness is complete. Second, the ground is level at the foot of the cross. None of us are more or less deserving of God's mercy.

It's true that if God kept a record, none of us could stand in His presence because we all have fallen short of God's perfect standard of holiness. This awareness of our own sinfulness shouldn't fill us with shame. Instead, let's live with gratitude for His gift of grace.

Thank You, Father, for Your grace and forgiveness.
Soften my heart, and help me release any
records of wrongs I've been keeping.

73

Psalm 119:37

Turn away

my *eyes* from

looking at

worthless things.

WORTHLESS THINGS

We've all heard the saying, "You are what you eat." Scripture has something similar. The people in the Old Testament became what they chased. Specifically, God's people chased false gods and became false themselves (2 Kings 17:15). God warned them that these idols were empty of power and compassion. By turning their attentions and affections toward them, the people became the same.

The path to the worship of false gods is a gradual one in most instances. Something worldly catches our eyes and, before we know it, our hearts begin to turn. The writer of the prayer found in Psalm 119 was aware of this truth. He asked the Lord to turn his gaze away from worthless things. Just like the children of Israel, we will become like the thing or person we worship. Our desire should be to become more and more like Christ, so we must fix our eyes on Him.

What tends to capture our gaze or attention? What do we chase after? If we are captivated by worldly things, we will begin to look like the world. But if we are concerned and consumed with the things of God, we will be conformed into the image of His Son.

Lord, help us to fix our gaze on You. Anything
or anyone else is a worthless thing.

74

Jonah 2:1–2

Then *Jonah* prayed to
the Lord his God from
the fish's *belly*. And
he said: "I cried out
to the *Lord* because
of my affliction, and
He *answered* me."

BECAUSE OF MY AFFLICTION

*W*hen do we find ourselves the closest to God? In what circumstances are we most likely to cry out to Him or seek Him? For most of us, it is often a season of affliction that drives us to our knees. When we've reached the end of our rope and don't know what else to do, we turn to God. This was certainly the case for Jonah.

Jonah was given a mission and a message by God. He was sent to preach to the people of Nineveh, but he didn't want to go there. So, he disobeyed and fled in the opposite direction. But as is always the case, he couldn't hide from the Lord, and disobedience always leads to discomfort. Jonah's affliction caused him to turn back toward God.

Troubles and trials are inevitable in this life. If we allow them, they can drive us closer to God than any season of ease ever could. We find, in those moments, that God's grace is sufficient (2 Corinthians 12:9). It doesn't matter if the affliction is, like Jonah's, directly connected to our disobedience or just part of living in a fallen world. We will find that God answers when we cry out to Him.

> Lord, may I have a humble heart that allows
> my affliction to drive me closer to You.

75

2 Kings 19:15

Then Hezekiah *prayed*
before the LORD, and said:
"O LORD God of Israel, the
One who dwells between the
cherubim, You are God, You
alone, of all the *kingdoms*
of the earth. You have
made *heaven* and earth."

YOU ARE GOD

*M*any of us would probably confess that our prayers sometimes lack a little enthusiasm. We find ourselves praying the same old words about the same old things. If we aren't careful, we can treat prayer like just another box to be checked off of our to-do lists. What if the passion of our prayers reflected the power of our God?

Hezekiah prayed passionate prayers because he knew the power of his God. It is evident in the way he addressed the Lord in the opening of this prayer. He didn't approach God casually, but with an awareness of and appreciation for His holiness and power.

In this prayer, Hezekiah acknowledged three things that he knew to be true of the One to whom he was praying. First, he knew that God was, in fact, God. "You are God," he prayed. Second, he declared that God was God "alone." Finally, he confessed that God was the creator of all that was in the heavens and earth.

It matters that we grasp the magnitude of who hears our prayers. He is God and He is God alone. He is the One who slung the stars across the sky and breathed life into man. He dwells in heaven and sits on the throne.

Praise You, Lord, that You are the One
who hears the cries of our hearts.

76

Psalm 119:11

Your *word* I have
hidden in my *heart*,
that I might not
sin against You.

HIDDEN TRUTH

What is the one piece of advice you've received the most in your life? The one where you can still hear the person's voice inside your head? For some of us, it's the voice of a parent telling us to drive safely or make good choices. Maybe we were blessed with a teacher who always encouraged us to do our best work.

My children say that even when I'm not around, they can hear my voice saying, "Don't be that person." It's true; I say it a lot. When someone is unkind, ungracious, or impatient, the words come out. When someone is selfish, greedy, or unforgiving, there it comes again. "Don't be that person." Trust me, there are plenty of opportunities to use it.

This is the idea behind the psalmist's prayer. He had intentionally meditated on Scripture and hidden God's Word in his heart so that at the appropriate times he would be reminded of God's instructions. He couldn't trust his own feelings or the world's opinion to help him do the right thing. It had to be the voice of God echoing in his heart and mind.

Help us, Father, to hide Your Word in our hearts. May we be so familiar with it that it immediately comes to mind and prevents us from sinning against You.

77

Psalm 122:6-7

Pray for the *peace*
of Jerusalem: "May
they *prosper* who *love*
you. Peace be within
your walls, prosperity
within your *palaces*."

PEACE AND PROSPERITY

Our communities may not have much in common. The average income, local cuisine, or geographical features may be different. It may seem that there isn't much common ground on which we can meet. But this prayer of David's for the city of Jerusalem highlights something we all desire for the places in which we live: peace and prosperity.

We need to love our communities. We are called to seek the welfare of the cities where God has placed us (Jeremiah 29:7). There are three ways we can begin to do just that.

Unbelievers sometimes operate in the world differently than we do. Claiming our communities for Christ may simply mean engaging in conversation with someone who uses language we wouldn't use. It means getting to know someone who looks, thinks, or acts differently from us. We have to get to know them so that they can get to know Him.

Be present in the community. Support local businesses, prayer-walk the streets, and be intentional about meeting the neighbors. Be seen on the streets and in the stores.

Scripture tells us that love covers a multitude of sins. This is also true of chicken soup and other meals made with love. Look around the community; who haven't you met yet? They could use a homemade meal or a batch of your favorite freshly baked goods.

> Lord show me how to become a bringer of peace and a beacon of prosperity to fill our homes and towns with You love and light.

78

Nehemiah 6:9

For they all were trying
to make us afraid, saying,
"Their *hands* will be
weakened in the *work*,
and it will not be done."
Now therefore, O God,
strengthen my hands.

STRENGTHEN MY HANDS

There will be times when God calls us to a specific task and we, unfortunately, encounter people who don't want us to succeed. If you've ever been in that situation then you know how discouraging it can be to face opposition to something you know you're supposed to do. It's even worse if someone openly mocks your efforts.

This is the situation Nehemiah found himself in as he went about the work of repairing the wall around Jerusalem. The enemy didn't want the work to be successful, and they made several attempts to interrupt or completely stop Nehemiah from completing his task. One specific tactic was to attempt to convince the workers that they were simply not capable of doing what they were trying to do. "You're not strong enough to do it," they said. "This work will not get done."

The ultimate aim of the enemy was to make the people so afraid of failing that they would quit and not risk the public humiliation. Nehemiah didn't retaliate with insults of his own. Instead, Nehemiah prayed to God for the strength to continue and complete the task.

If God has called us to a specific task or area of ministry, He will give us the strength to complete it. When the Enemy taunts us, let us turn to God.

Father, help me to hear Your voice clearly as You call me to action, and give me strength to comple the tasks.

79

Psalm 25:5

Lead me in Your *truth*
and teach me, for
You are the God of
my *salvation*; on You
I wait all the day.

PATIENCE

*I*t's often been said that one should never ask God for patience. I assume the logic is that He would then make you wait for something. The truth is, however, that waiting is nothing new. We are all familiar with waiting, as were the men and women in Scripture. Abraham waited on his promised heir. Noah waited for the floods to subside. The father waited on his prodigal son to come home. People have been waiting since the beginning of time.

There are lessons that can only be learned in the waiting, and we must trust in God's timing. So often, though, we want to rush things. We sense God working in a certain area, and we want to jump in and hurry it along. We feel prepared to play a part in the game, but instead find ourselves sitting on the bench waiting our turn.

We're like the children of Israel waiting on Moses to come back down from the mountain or the disciples in the upper room waiting on the Holy Spirit to come down. We know something good is coming, and the anticipation is almost more than we can bear.

I don't know what you're waiting on, friend, but we're all waiting on something. Let's wait well. Let's wait faithfully for the One who promises—as Jesus did—to return to us (John 14:3).

Lord, Your timing is perfect. Create in
me a new and patient heart.

80

Psalm 139:9-10

If I take the *wings* of
the morning, and dwell
in the uttermost parts
of the *Sea*, even there
Your hand shall *lead*
me, and Your right
hand shall *hold* me.

EVEN THERE

*I*t's not difficult for some of us to get lost. One missed turn, one moment of distraction, or one detour is all it takes for some of us to end up far from our intended destination. The GPS has been a huge blessing to many of us, allowing us to course-correct when we've wandered off the path.

As David prayed the words of Psalm 139, he pondered all the places he could potentially find himself. What if he ascended all the way to heaven? What if he found himself all the way to the grave? Or the uttermost parts of the sea? Or covered in complete darkness? What then?

Even then, David concluded, the Lord would be near. He trusted that no matter how off-course he found himself, God would still see him and lead him back. He could never wander too far from his heavenly Father. Not death, distance, nor darkness could prevent God's saving right hand.

We can take comfort in knowing that the same God who could see David wherever he roamed watches over us today. No matter where we find ourselves, God can lead us out even from there. No matter how deep the pit, His hand will hold us close.

Thank You, Lord, that we are always in Your presence and within Your reach.

81

Psalm 23:4

Yea, though I walk through the *Valley* of the shadow of death, I will fear no evil; for *You* are with me; Your rod and Your staff, they *comfort* me.

WALK THROUGH THE VALLEY

*A*ccording to several articles I've read recently, the fear of death and the process of dying is one of the most common fears. *Death Anxiety* is a newly coined term, but the idea is nothing new. As Solomon said in Ecclesiastes, "There is nothing new under the sun" (Ecclesiastes 1:9).

David was intimately acquainted with the fears surrounding death. He had faced predators as a shepherd and powerful enemies as a king. Yet he knew that even in the valley of the shadow of death, God was with him.

We have the same comfort today. Jesus suffered and died so that he "might taste death for everyone" (Hebrews 2:9). By experiencing and conquering death, he delivered "all those who *through fear of death* were subject to lifelong slavery" (v. 15 ESV, emphasis added). We no longer have to fear death. The prophet instructed the children of Israel to not fear what other people feared (Isaiah 8:12).

We will all, at some point, journey through the valley ourselves for it is appointed for each man to die (Hebrews 9:27). Whether we are experiencing it ourselves or watching someone we love experience it, David reminds us that we don't need to have any fear. We won't take a single step of the journey alone. We will always have the presence and the comfort of our Shepherd.

Thank You, Father, for being ever-present by
my side and for taking away my fears.

82

Psalm 51:7

Purge me with *hyssop*,
and I shall be *clean*;
wash me, and I shall
be *whiter* than snow.

PURGE ME WITH HYSSOP

David desired that a thorough cleansing from the Lord take place in his life. He didn't want to simply be white-washed and have the appearance of cleanliness. He prayed that God would purge him of impurities. This process can be painful, but it is necessary in the life of every believer. We don't want sin to linger. It needs to be removed by any means necessary.

In the gospel of John, it's described as pruning. "Every branch in Me that does not bear fruit He takes away" (John 15:2). What would it look like if we were pruned of everything that did not bear gospel fruit? Every activity. Every relation-ship. Everything we call ministry that is really self-promotion. Every pedestal we have created for ourselves. Every act of service that has served to distract us from the Savior.

What if we were purged of everything that wasn't of God. What if anything that didn't bring God glory was wiped away? How much of our time, money, and energy is spent on things that don't spread the gospel, make disciples, or cause us to love our neighbors more?

Sometimes the branches don't fall easily and the purg-ing is painful. It's okay. God knows what He's doing, and when He is done, we shall be whiter than snow.

Cleanse me, Father, of any impurities. Give me the courage to prune those things that no longer bear fruit.

83

Psalm 16:5-6

O LORD, You are the *portion* of my *inheritance* and my cup; You maintain my lot. The lines have fallen to me in *pleasant* places; yes, I have a *good* inheritance.

A GOOD INHERITANCE

What is the most precious item you've ever received following a loved one's passing? It may have been a piece of jewelry, a handmade item, or some old photographs. Sometimes an inheritance can include a large sum of money or a parcel of land.

David would have been very familiar with the concept of inheritance. Being royalty, a great deal was passed from one generation to the next, including titles, blessings, and wealth. In his day, battles were fought and relationships ruined over the divvying up of possessions.

David's prayer showed what he considered most valuable. It wasn't his throne, title, or palace. The Lord was his inheritance, and David considered that a good thing. An old pastor once said, "If there was no heaven, I would have loved Jesus anyway." David would have certainly echoed that sentiment.

We too have a beautiful inheritance in Christ. One of the many blessings promised to those who endure is "the bright and morning star" (Revelation 22:16; 2:28). Christ is our portion, our good inheritance.

Thank You, Lord, for my inheritance in You.

84

Psalm 141:3

Set a *guard*,
O LORD, over my
mouth; keep
watch over the
door of my *lips*.

GUARD MY MOUTH

*C*ouldn't we all pray these exact words multiple times a day? We've all allowed words to escape our lips that we immediately regretted. Other words, if not regretted immediately, have certainly come back to haunt us. Words have the uncanny capacity to hurt or to heal.

David prayed that the Lord would set a guard over his mouth. He wanted God to be the One to determine what words he spoke and to help him refrain from any unnecessary speech. Wouldn't it be nice if we all desired that?

Paul also knew the dangers of misused words. He instructed the church at Ephesus to use only those words that uplifted the hearers and were appropriate for the situation (Ephesians 4:29). Paul's guidelines—uplifting and fitting the occasion—would still be a great litmus test for us to use before speaking.

Imagine pausing, especially during stressful or emotional circumstances, and weighing our words before spewing them out. Will our words serve to benefit, uplift, and encourage the person hearing them? And are our words appropriate for the situation and audience? If not, may the Lord give us the wisdom to not speak them.

Father, give me wisdom and grace to speak only
those words that are pleasing to Your ear.

85

Luke 23:34

"Father, *forgive*
them, for they
do not *know*
what they do."

FATHER, FORGIVE THEM

*W*hat is the hardest thing you've ever had to forgive? Something probably immediately popped into your mind. We've all been wounded by someone, and it can take a while for the pain to ease. If we're honest, most of us still have some forgiving that we need to do; it takes time.

Imagine if you can, Jesus on the cross. As he gasped for air and writhed in pain, He prayed. He didn't pray for the pain to end or for angels to descend. He didn't ask God to hurl lightning bolts at the jeering crowd. Jesus, from the cross, prayed that God would forgive the very ones who hung Him there.

It's a perfect example of praying for our enemies while practicing the art of forgiveness. Jesus didn't make it look easy because He knew it wouldn't be easy for us. He also wouldn't want us to confuse forgiving someone with condoning their behavior. To say, "I forgive you," is not the same as saying, "It's okay." It's an important difference, and one that Jesus so poignantly illustrates.

Thank You, Lord, for Your example of forgiveness
and also for the forgiveness we have received. Help
us to also forgive those who have wronged us.

86

Exodus 2:23

Now it happened in the process of *time* that the king of Egypt died. Then the *children* of Israel groaned because of the bondage, and they *cried* out; and their cry came up to *God* because of the bondage.

A WORDLESS PRAYER

There are all types of prayers. There are the flowery, eloquent ones we may hear at official events. There are the simple, earnest, heartwarming prayers heard around dinner tables. There are prayers of praise and prayers of penitence. And then there are wordless prayers. The ones we have all poured out when at those times in our lives when the grief was too great.

When the children of Israel were being enslaved and mistreated, they were in such despair that they were able to only groan. But their cries were no less a prayer than any other. Those cries went up, and God heard them.

There are times when we simply don't know what to pray. Maybe the need is so great or the pain too intense. Or perhaps we are confused over a situation and aren't sure which outcome to seek. In those moments, the Spirit intercedes and lifts up prayers on our behalf (Romans 8:26).

We thank You, Lord, that You always hear the prayer
of a sincere heart. Whether it be shouts of praise,
whispers of confession, or groanings too great
for words, our cries always reach Your ears.

87

Judges 1:1

Now after the death of
Joshua it came to pass that
the *children* of Israel asked
the Lord, saying, "*Who*
shall be *first* to go up for
us against the Canaanites
to *fight* against them?"

PRAYER FOR DIRECTION

How often do we seek the Lord's guidance in the decisions that we must make? Do we spend time in prayer when we must choose a place of employment, or a spouse, or the proper medical treatment? We would certainly be wise to do so, but often we get caught up in other things. We check with our family, friends, and feelings. We examine how the decision looks on paper or whether we think it makes sense.

After the death of Joshua, with no new leader apparently appointed, the children of Israel sought direction from the Lord. They needed to know which tribe should lead the way into battle. God heard their prayers and gave them the guidance they needed.

David also made a practice of seeking counsel from the Lord (2 Samuel 2:1). On multiple occasions, he prayed before advancing on an enemy. There were also moments in Scripture when people failed to seek God (Isaiah 31:1), and the results were not so favorable.

God knows what is best for His people. He knows every path we take and where those paths lead. Let's be quick to seek His counsel so that we may follow His will for our lives. And when His direction surprises us, let's trust that He knows best how to lead us into the battle.

Lord, I seek Your guidance as I take new steps each day. May each step I take be closer to You.

88

Psalm 71:24

My *tongue* also
shall *talk* of Your
righteousness all
the day long.

OUR TESTIMONY

$\mathcal{I}$f you've ever taken a training class or attended a seminar on sales, they will teach you one thing about making someone comfortable: get them talking about what is important to them. For some it may be their families. Others may love to talk about their hobbies. We can tell a lot about a person by the things they choose to—or refuse to—discuss.

What would someone be able to tell about us if they spent a day in our company? They would probably know if we were married, had kids, or our occupation. We may even get into deeper topics like where we grew up or where we go to church. Just imagine all that you could learn about someone if you spent an entire day with them.

The author of the prayer found in Psalm 71 declared that he would speak of the Lord's righteousness all day long. He praised God for being his hope and trust since his youth (v. 5). Praises filled his mouth the whole day. How wonderful to have that be our testimony—to praise the righteousness of God all day long!

Let's make it a point to share the goodness of our God with the people around us. We have plenty of things to praise Him about in our lives. If someone who didn't know the Lord spent the day with us, would they hear about Him from our lips?

Thank You, Father, for Your abundance of
blessings in my life. Help me to be a blessing
in the lives of those around me.

89

Isaiah 25:4

For *You* have been a
strength to the poor, a
strength to the needy
in his distress, a *refuge*
from the storm, a
shade from the heat.

STRENGTH, SAFETY, AND SHADE

*W*e all have different stories regarding our walk with the Lord. Our journeys through the valleys may have taken different amounts of time, and some of us may have weathered the storm better than others. But if we all sat down and shared our testimonies with one another, we would probably see some common themes.

In Isaiah's prayer, he described three things that he had seen about the Lord over the course of his lifetime. First, God had been a source of strength for people who were poor, needy, and in distress. If we have not already experienced poverty, need, or distress in our lives, we certainly will, and it is the Lord' strength that will bring us through.

Second, God had proven to be a source of safety in the storm. Whether the storm was a health battle, a financial struggle, a relationship unraveling, or something completely different, the Lord is the refuge for His people.

Finally, Isaiah said that God had been a shade from the heat. Is there any sweeter relief than stepping into the shade and escaping the heat of the day? The idea of shade calls to mind images of rest and solace, and that is what the Lord is for His people.

> Thank You, Lord, for being all of these things
> to us. You are and always have been the
> strength, safety, and shade for Your people.

90

Revelation 22:20

Amen.

Even so, *come*, Lord Jesus!

COME, LORD JESUS!

"*C*ome, Lord Jesus!" is often uttered following a tragedy of some sort. Our hearts long for our Savior when life is difficult. People can be exhausting. New wounds are inflicted or old pains resurface. Sometimes the longing for a loved one becomes too much. And so we pray, "Come, Lord Jesus!"

Sometimes we become weary of the way people choose cruelty over kindness and grudges over grace. Forgiveness feels foreign, and the world seems cold. We long for peace, but others are for war (Psalm 120:7). And so we pray, "Come, Lord Jesus!"

Then we begin to wonder. *Why does He not come?* In our ignorance, it seems cruel for Him to linger. We long for Him to swoop in and save the day. We want the pain to end, the frauds to be exposed, and the truth revealed.

Jesus will return for His children, coming like a thief in the night (1 Thessalonians 5:2), so let us be ready. Each day the Lord tarries is another twenty-four-hour period giving someone else yet another opportunity to repent and believe. There are still those who don't know Jesus. And don't we all have friends, family, and neighbors who—if He returned today—would spend eternity without Him?. Let's be busy about our Father's business, ensuring that others are ready for His return.

> Lord, I invite You to come into my life and
> help me to choose kindness over cruelty,
> faith over fear, and love over judgment.

91

Psalm 119:15

I will *meditate*

on Your

precepts, and

contemplate

Your ways.

ATTITUDE BEFORE ACTION

There are things that we, as Christ followers, are called to do. There are physical actions that we are to take. We are to care for widows and orphans. We are to show hospitality. There is much work to be done, but we can't just head out into the world unprepared.

Our actions and our efforts will be fruitful only if our attitudes are correct. In Psalm 119, the psalmist prayed that he would meditate on the precepts and ways of the Lord. He understood that the hard work of the gospel began with getting his mind focused on the things of God. It's a truth that still applies to us today.

Peter also taught believers the same concept when he instructed believers to prepare their minds for action (1 Peter 1:13). Jesus Himself taught the importance of counting the cost, of planning and preparing before building a tower or going to war (Luke 14:28–31). All throughout Scripture, there are reminders of the necessity of mentally preparing ourselves prior to taking action.

Let's meditate on the Words of God so that we are able to accomplish the works of God assigned to us.

Thank You, Lord, for Your precepts that serve
to teach, train, prepare, and encourage us.

92

Psalm 119:38

Establish Your *word*
to Your servant,
who is *devoted*
to fearing You.

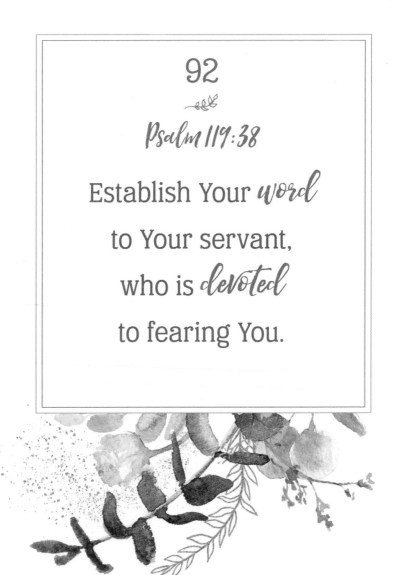

WHOLLY DEVOTED

There is really only one way to live out this faith journey: we must be wholly devoted. There can be no option of backing out when times become difficult. David had this kind of devotion, and he readily attested to the fact that all his goodness meant nothing apart from the Lord. God desires wholehearted devotion.

The first mention of Peter in Scripture is when he is called by Jesus, along with his brother, to be a disciple. We are told that he immediately left his nets and followed Him (Matthew 4:18–20). Those nets represented his very livelihood—and a lucrative one at that. But one encounter with Jesus, and Peter was all in. There wasn't a probationary period, a plan B, or a polling of the crowd for public opinion.

Jesus demands nothing less of us today. We must follow Him completely and hold nothing of ourselves back. We must be all in like Peter and devoted like the psalmist. A lukewarm follower is detestable to God (Revelation 3:16).

Father, give us the boldness to drop everything and follow when You call. Let us not put anything before You or cling to anything besides You. Establish Your word in us for we are devoted to fearing and following You.

93

Psalm 119:33

Teach me,
O Lord, the
way of Your
statutes, and
I shall keep
it to the end.

OBEDIENCE

God made His expectations very clear to the people: "walk in my statutes and observe my commandments and do them" (Leviticus 26:3 ESV). He also made clear the blessings they could expect if they were obedient. He promised peace, fruitful labor, and His presence among them. God essentially said "If you obey me, this is what you can expect."

On the other hand, God also laid out the consequences for disobedience. They could expect to experience panic, heartache, labor done in vain, and God to set His face against them. While the blessings for obedience were clearly stated, the punishments for disobedience were also made clear.

While obedience would bring peace to the people, disobedience would bring panic. If you have ever tried to operate outside of God's will for your life, you have likely experienced this for yourself. Your days lacked peace, and your efforts didn't produce the desired results.

We can best show our love for God by obeying Him (John 14:15). In return, God fills us with peace, multiplies the effects of our efforts, and makes His presence known. May our prayer be the same as the psalmist:

> Teach us Your ways, O Lord, and we
> will keep them to the end.

94

Nehemiah 1:5

And I said: "I pray, LORD
God of heaven, O *great*
and *awesome* God, You
who keep Your *covenant*
and *mercy* with those
who *love* You and observe
Your commandments."

PRAY WITH PASSION

For many of us, prayer time can lack emotion. It can become nothing more than the reading of a list of current needs with an occasional "thank You" thrown in for good measure. Take a moment and read Hannah's prayer (1 Samuel 2). Read it out loud to really get a feel for it.

Do you hear the reverence for the character of God? The awe for what He had done? This is prayer with passion.

If your prayer life has grown a little stale, spend some time studying the prayers of people throughout Scripture. Prayers like:

- David praying for deliverance in Psalm 3.
- Paul's prayers for the Ephesians in Ephesians 1:15–23.
- Jesus' prayer of submission in Luke 22:39–46.

Pay close attention to these prayers—to not only what they said to God, but what they said about Him. If prayer has become drudgery for you, ask God to restore to you the joy of your salvation.

Thank You, Father, for the privilege of prayer. May we not take for granted our access to You. Instead, may we always praise You, God, for hearing us when we call.

95

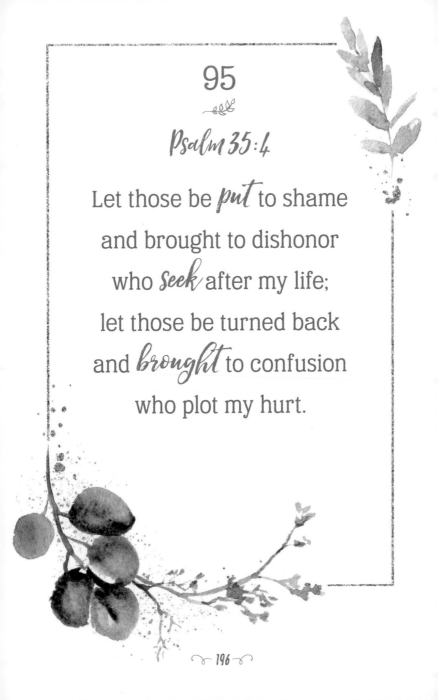

Psalm 35:4

Let those be *put* to shame
and brought to dishonor
who *seek* after my life;
let those be turned back
and *brought* to confusion
who plot my hurt.

CONFUSION FOR OUR ENEMIES

There is a lot of chaos and confusion in the world. But this should not make us believe that things are spiraling out of control. It is God who creates and controls calamity (Isaiah 45:7).

A perfect example of an enemy being thrown into confusion is the plagues that God sent into Egypt. Frogs covered the land. Gnats appeared everywhere. Then flies took over, and livestock began dying. Hail rained from the sky. And there was certainly confusion.

In the midst of the swirling drama, God said something that can give us hope in today's chaotic world. The Lord promised to make a distinction between the livestock of Israel and the livestock of Egypt (Exodus 9:4). What looked like chaos was perfectly clear and calm to the Lord. Nothing was spinning out of control.

The same God who created an orderly universe and brings calm to His people, can send our enemies into confusion. Remember, God made it clear that He was the One who had put Pharaoh in power to begin with. Trust Him to be in control.

Lord, You are in control. I pray for calmness and clarity
in what is often a confusing and chaotic world.

96

Psalm 27:1

The LORD is my *light* and my salvation; whom shall I fear? The LORD is the *strength* of my life; of whom shall I be afraid?"

NO FEAR

*W*e don't know what the future holds, what losses await us, or what trials are looming around the bend. We can't know what struggles we will soon encounter or what heartache is yet to happen. What we can be assured of is the Lord's presence in our lives.

The first words the angel ever spoke to a teenaged girl named Mary were, "The Lord is with you" (Luke 1:28).

The very next statement was, "Do not be afraid" (v. 30). Only after these two statements did the angel tell Mary what was about to happen. Imagine the angel speaking with tenderness to a young, innocent girl: "Mary, the Lord is with you, and you do not need to be afraid."

Why did she not have to be afraid? Because the Lord was with her. And it was through that lens that she was able to view what the angel was about to tell her. We see this same pairing of statements in Isaiah 41:10: "Fear not, for I am with you." Don't be afraid. Why? Because God is with you.

There are many unknowns in life. And life is full of so many things that can blindside us and catch us unaware. But we know what we need to know and, like Mary, we can choose to view all other things in light of these two statements: The Lord is with you. Do not be afraid.

Father, I don't know what tomorrow holds,
but I put my faith and trust in You.

97

Lamentations 3:19

Remember my
affliction and *roaming*,
the wormwood
and the *gall*.

REMEMBER MY AFFLICTION

This prayer was a plea by a prophet for the Lord to remember his affliction. Can't we all relate? Something within us needs to know that our pain is not in vain. We take comfort in the knowledge that the Lord sees every tear.

Paul was beaten with rods three times, stoned, and shipwrecked three times. He faced danger from rivers, bandits, fellow Jews, false believers, and Gentiles. Affliction awaited him in the city, the country, and at sea. He labored, toiled, and went without sleep. He experienced hunger, thirst, cold, and nakedness (2 Corinthians 11:25–27).

Paul described his afflictions as light and momentary while still in the midst of them. Paul was beheaded in Rome; he wasn't writing this letter while safely tucked away in retirement and reflecting. How was he able to have such a perspective?

He viewed everything in light of eternity. Paul didn't say that earthly troubles are light and momentary. He said they are light and momentary compared with the glory that awaits us.

Jesus approached the cross the same way: "who for the joy that was set before Him endured the cross" (Hebrews 12:2). He faced the cross with an eye on the joy to come.

Lord, remember our afflictions that we have endured in Your name, but give us an eternal perspective on them. Though we may experience heartache here on earth, one day we will stand in Your presence and deem our afflictions not even worth mentioning.

98

Psalm 73:24

You will *guide*
me with Your
counsel, and
afterward receive
me to *glory*.

AFTERWARD

*T*rials can often seem so overwhelming that we think they'll never end. You'd give almost anything to see a light at the end of the tunnel when you're up to your neck in the drama. The Lord told Abram that his offspring would experience affliction for four hundred years, but that afterward they would come out with great possessions and be given the promised land.

Sometimes we have to remind ourselves that there is an *afterward* for those who love the Lord. What we see here and the pain we feel here is heartbreaking. The loss, betrayal, and confusion hurts. It hurts, just like four hundred years of affliction hurts. But we are also promised an afterward.

Paul was certain "that the sufferings of this present time are not worth comparing with the glory that is to be revealed to us" (Romans 8:18 esv). Yes, there is pain, but there is an afterward. There are valleys, but we're just passing through (Psalm 23:4).

The afflictions don't seem light and momentary right now, but that's because we aren't in the afterward yet. It's coming because He is coming, and it will happen in the twinkling of an eye. Then all the suffering will fade from our memories as we enjoy *afterward*.

Thank You, Lord, that I have the hope of an afterward
and Your promise of eternal life in Your kingdom.

99

Psalm 80:3

Restore us, O
God; cause
Your face to
shine, and we
shall be saved!

JOY RESTORED

*W*e have all experienced periods where we lacked peace or joy due to some area of disobedience in our lives. It's our own fault, and we know it. The beauty of a relationship with God is that He is always willing to forgive and restore.

We read passages like Jeremiah 25, see the Lord speaking persistently and the people not listening, and we can totally relate. When this scenario happens in Scripture, there is normally a passage that begins with "therefore," which lists the consequences of the people's behavior.

One of the consequences that the people suffered during this bout of disobedience was the removal of their joy (v. 10). But with God, restoration is available. God said that the people just needed to call to Him. They didn't have to fix themselves or undo their mistakes. No one had to become good enough or try to climb their way back to Him.

Then, when they called, He we would answer them. He would heal, restore, cleanse, and forgive them. But that wasn't all. He promised to restore their joy. Joy restored is a beautiful thing. When we fail and disobey, let's learn to repent quickly and return to the joy of the Lord.

Lord, I'm grateful that even though my life is not perfect, I am able to find joy and peace in You.

100

Psalm 8:3

When I consider Your
heavens, the work of
Your fingers, the *moon*
and the *stars*, which
You have ordained.

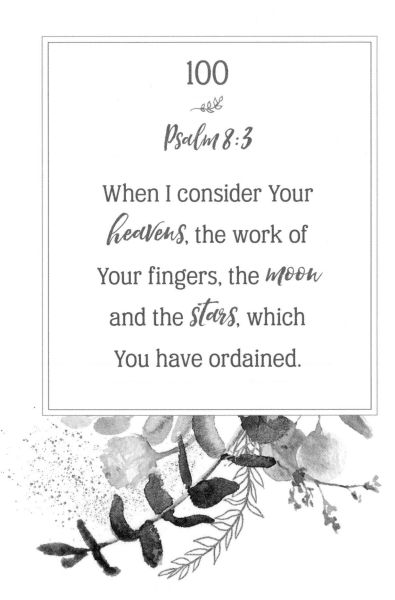